Evolution of Democracy. The Assassination of President JFK SOLVED

"Gentlemen, when a minister sets himself above the laws, as Mr. Perceval did, he does it at his [own] risk. If this were not so, the mere will of the minister would become the law, and what would then become of your liberties?

I trust that this serious lesson will operate as a warning to all future ministers and that they will henceforth do the right thing, for if the upper ranks of society are permitted to act wrong with impunity, the inferior ramifications will soon become wholly corrupted."

John Bellingham May 1812

David Gomadza

Tomorrow's World Order

No wish of a leader can be allowed to become law. Otherwise, if that happens then it means erasing hard-earned liberties.

The Beast.

It will take another evil act for humanity to fully understand what democracy all is about.

Don't get me wrong, I want a democratic society. A society where no one is above the law. Where a "minister's will does NOT become the law".

A society where the Mighty might fall at the hands of the common man if he is in the wrong.

A society where there is fear of the rule of law.

But the Beast, I think, is the greatest threat to democracy. Simply because the Beast does everything for 'personal gains.'

But who is the Beast?

I can tell you outright that every event shocking or horrific for the past two centuries is the work of the Beast.

Yes, think of any event. Surely there is a Beast behind it.

The Beast has found it rewarding and interesting to determine the course of history.

Yes, the Beast is running the show. All major evil events are the works of the Beast.

All wars, all terrorist attacks, 9/11 in America, July 7 in Britain, and all assassinations; the assassination of JFK, and recently the Russia and Ukraine War are all the works of the Beast.

I will tell you first how the Beast is doing this.

This Beast to gain a competitive advantage is recreating history.

Over the decades, the Beast has collected all the scripts of past events. Now what it is doing is simply going back in time and recreating that event. Event by event.

Would you be surprised if I tell you that the current Russia-Ukraine war is a 'film' based on the Second Anglo-Dutch war of 1665-1667?

Event by event date by date?

Check out our prediction. [links inside.]

But I must give the Beast credit in the Assassination of John F. Kennedy, for the Beast tried hard to be very clever to disguise everything, so that everything looks like just another evil act by a deranged one-man assassin.

But we finally opened the Pandora.

I can tell you that the assassination of JFK was a pre-planned cold-blood murder plan.

It was an execution.

Whether this assassination of JFK took the evolution of democracy to another stage is not to be discussed in this book; I will cover this in volume II. Firstly, I will prove beyond doubt that the assassination of JFK was an event based on a carefully planned script but a murder plan.

Even though Lee Harvey Oswald might have pulled the trigger. The Beast was the mastermind.

Even though history repeats itself; lightning does not strike twice in one place.

The Beast combined three scripts of the evilest crimes in the history of mankind and superimposed all events to produce one shocking, brutal event in the history of mankind.

SUPERIMPOSING OF THREE HORRIFIC CRIMES INTO ONE HORRIFIC EVENT.

This is the magic trick no one has ever thought possible but the Pandora we have opened.

That means three assassins are all present and all playing a major part to make sure that the assassination goes according to plan.

This means three major victims (mainly of the Mighty in power).

This means three crime scenes, but all combined into one huge confusing crime scene to fuel major conspiracy theories that last for centuries. But thanks to Tomorrow's World Order, we will show you that yes; this is one of the cold-calculated clever murder plans, but it is a crime that needs resolving and something we are going to do.

I don't want to spoil the excitement. I will just reiterate that ladies and gentlemen, we have three assassins all present in the JFK assassination.

We have all three victims in one crime scene.

We have all the evidence.

We have all the leads.

We have all the unbelievable explanations.

We have all the secrets and confusion.

Would you be surprised that for more than fifty years, still, no one had come up with an explanation that kills all conspiracy theories until now?

I tell you after reading this book you will never have a single question about what happened on that sad day in Dallas, Texas, on 22 November 1963.

But the only problem is that after putting the Beast out of business by revealing its secrets and murderous plan. It might start thinking about even a more complicated and horrific event that will create conspiracy theories for the next thousand years.

Word of advice; when reading the reader must have in mind three crime scenes superimposed into one. Lift one above the other, meaning you will have three layers of events; so you can see a three layer vertical cross-section.In the end, put all three layers into one and see all the actors of all three crime scenes at play in this Assassination of JFK.

In the end, every event makes sense. You can tell who was behind all this.

Surely you will realize and believe that the Beast exists.

Even though others killed and played parts, someone was making sure that everyone does what the Beast wanted.

The Beast made sure that everyone followed the superimposed scripts. The Beast is like the film director.

THE BEAST KILLED JFK.

But who is the Beast?

DEDICATION

Justice and Peace.

Evolution of Democracy. The Assassination of President JFK SOLVED.

ACKNOWLEDGMENTS

Tomorrow's World Order

"Gentlemen, when a minister sets himself above the laws, as Mr. Perceval did, he does it at his [own] risk. If this were not so, the mere will of the minister would become the law, and what would then become of your liberties?

I trust that this serious lesson will operate as a warning to all future ministers and that they will henceforth do the right thing, for if the upper ranks of society are permitted to act wrong with impunity, the inferior ramifications will soon become wholly corrupted."

John Bellingham May 1812

A combination of all high treason crimes into one the assassination of the President of the United States John F Kennedy 22 November 1963

The three victims.

King Charles I of England 30 January 1649.

The Prime Minister of England Spencer Perceval 11 May 1812

The President of the USA John F Kennedy 22 November 1963

The Killers

The killer of King Charles I: Hidden identity but likely Richard Brandon and his assistant who could be his father George for him and his assistant but to be resolved but played by Clint Hill who stood over the king after beheading him. A member of the secret service or representing the secret service in the assassination of JFK.

The killer of Spencer Perceval: John Bellingham, represented by the umbrella man in the assassination of JFK.

The "umbrella man", identified by the United States House Select Committee on Assassinations in 1978 as Louie Steven Witt, is a name given to a figure who appears in the Zapruder film, and several other films and photographs, near the Stemmons Freeway sign within Dealey Plaza during the assassination of United States President John F. Kennedy.

He was also one of the closest bystanders to President John F. Kennedy when Kennedy was first struck by a bullet. As Kennedy's limousine approached, the man opened up and lifted the umbrella high above his head, then spun or panned the umbrella from east to west (clockwise) as the president passed by him. In the aftermath of the assassination, the "umbrella man" sat down on the sidewalk next to another man ("Dark Complected Man") before getting up and walking towards the Texas School Book Depository. The fact that both men sat there so calmly after the shooting has raised suspicion.

This is exactly what the killer of the British prime minister John Bellingham did after shooting Spencer Perceval. He was so relaxed that he walked over and sat down on the bench.

But read with care. I said that the Beast is combining all three crime scenes into one. He is combining all the events in the other two; the beheading of Charles I and the assassination of Spencer Perceval to help carry out a perfect murder.

I think he was the signal-man to tell the shooter when to shoot for a perfect shot. So, he has a part to play.

But care must be taken in interpreting this. The Beast might have sent him to do what he did, but without shooting the president. He might have done this without knowing that another person summoned by the Beast was to shoot the president.

Early speculation came from assassination researchers Josiah

Thompson and Richard Sprague, who noticed the open umbrella in a series of photographs. Thompson and Sprague suggested that the "umbrella man" may have been acting as a signaler of some kind, opening his umbrella to signal "go ahead" and then raising it to communicate "fire a second round" to other gunmen.

Louie Steven Witt said that he brought the umbrella simply to heckle Kennedy, whose father, Joseph, had been a supporter of the Nazi-appeasing British Prime Minister Neville Chamberlain. By waving a black umbrella, Chamberlain's trademark fashion accessory, Witt said he was protesting the Kennedy family appeasing Adolf Hitler before World War II.

Wikipedia.

https://en.wikipedia.org/wiki/Umbrella_man_(JFK_assassination).

We also know that the executioner of Charles I, king of England, had assistance. We can also assume that the shooter, if Lee Harvey Oswald, had an assistant to signal when to take the shot.

Firstly, the King himself was his assistant as he was to help him know when to behead the king. The king was going to use his hand to signal the right time to strike.

The umbrella man could be another assistant in pinpointing exactly when to take the shot. This is because this Umbrella man opened the umbrella only when the president's limousine was in the position where the bullet hit the president. That can't be coincidental.

But he might have been told by the Beast to protest as he claimed and open the umbrella just as the president's limousine was passing him.

The beast will have told the shooter when to strike and to wait for a signal. When the shooter saw the umbrella, even if he was not told that it would be, an umbrella took the shot.

The umbrella man could be a diversion from the second shooter.

The Beast would want to recreate the beheading of Charles I. So he might have placed two killers one from the sixth floor of the Texas School Book Depository and the other one to match the front right impact when the king's head fell on the ground meaning the second shooter was in the Grass Knoll.

Having this in mind, therefore, the umbrella man was to give signals to two shooters at the same time to synchronize the shoots. This can make the two shooters all shoot at the same time.

This is in line with the script to make all the soldiers have the blood of the king on their clothes and unlock his locks. Instead of someone suspecting that the secret service had blood on their hands. Meaning that they were involved in the assassination of JFK.

This will enable them to have the president's blood on their clothes.

The executioner dropped the king's head into the crowd and the soldiers swarmed around it, dipping their handkerchiefs in his blood and cutting off locks of his hair.

https://en.wikipedia.org/wiki/Execution_of_Charles_I

On his execution King Charles I spoke to a Gentleman.

"Then turning to a Gentleman whose cloak he observed to touch the edge of the Ax, he said unto him, Hurt not the Ax, meaning by blunting the edge thereof,"

https://quod.lib.umich.edu/e/eebo/A40615.0001.001/1:6?rgn=div1;
view=fulltext.

"Whose clock he observed,"

The umbrella, considering what is said the Umbrella man has done, might represent the cloak the king observed.

Colonel Hacker.

Colonel Francis Hacker (died 19 October 1660) was an English soldier who fought for Parliament during the English Civil War and was one of the Regicides of King Charles I of England.

During the trial of Charles I, Hacker was one of the officers specially charged with the custody of the King, and usually commanded the guard of halberdiers which escorted Charles to and from Westminster Hall. He was one of the three officers to whom the warrant for the King's execution was addressed, was present himself on the scaffold, supervised the execution, and signed the order to the executioner. [8] According to Herbert, he treated the King respectfully.

The warrant for the execution of the King had been in Hacker's possession.

Colonel Hacker led the King forth on the day of his execution, followed by the bishop of London.

Hacker was sentenced to death and was hanged at Tyburn on 19 October 1660.

Wikipedia.

Then [the king] turning to Colonel Hacker, he said. "Take care, they do not put me in pain."

The Magic Bullet.

Hacking of the President during the time he lived in Britain from 1938 to 1939.

I have looked at the possibility that JFK's death was a result of the hacking by the British, something that led others to believe that he was a traitor selling the country to foreigners. A puppet of the British. This can also explain the speech about the enemies within. Something echoed by his brother as well. How can he tell the Americans that he was hacked [chipped whilst young] and the British listen to all his conversations etc? Something Lyndon Johnson might have suspected and accused him of treason.

The hacking might have been said to be part of his medical records.

Having said that, there is another theory.

The Magic Bullet.

We know that it is possible

for hacking [chipping] with an implant of a miniature rotary propeller in the lumbar bone whilst still young can be used as an internal gun that uses pressure to explode parts of the body. The implant is used to work using pressure build-up that can explode at chosen parts of the body through zoning to act like a bullet. Hence the magic bullet.

This can explain the fact that this acted like the second gunman.

Lee Harvey Oswald might have fired the deadly shots, but the Beast used the magic bullet from the implanted chip to explode his head at the same time.

The Executioner.

Then the King turning to the Executioner, said, "I shall say but very short prayers, and when I stretch forth my hands — Then the King called to Doctor Juxon for his Night-cap, and having put it on, he said to the Executioner: Will my hair trouble you?"

The king managed to put his hair in the nightcap given to him by William Juxon with the help of the Executioner and the Bishop.

The King then said unto the Executioner, is my hair as it should be?

looking on the Block, he said unto the Executioner, you should make it to be steddie.

The king went on to say; When I shall stretch forth my hands in this manner, then—

After that, when standing, he had spoken two or three words unto himself, with his hands, and eyes lifted towards Heaven, immediately stooping down, he laid his neck upon the Block, and when the Executioner had again put all his hair under his cap. The King said, Stay till I give the Sign.

Executioner.

So, I do, if it pleases your Majesty; and after a very little respite, the King did stretch forth his hands, and immediately the Executioner, at one blow, did sever his head from his Body.

https://quod.lib.umich.edu/e/eebo/A40615.0001.001/1:6?rgn=div1; view=fulltext

The second shooter was from the Grassy Knoll.

The Beast must go by the script and find ways to recreate what happened to King Charles I. The king was beheaded by an axe. The murder weapons. So, the killer's murder weapon was an axe and was from the back as he faced down on the block. But his head suffered right front injuries from the beheading as it hit the floor.

The Beast to recreate this must find two shooters who shoot at the same time. One from the back, mainly the fatal shot and the other from the Grassy Knoll.

Policeman Joe Marshall Smith gave an account of running to the Grassy Knoll chasing after a suspected shooter. But when the person showed him his secret service credentials, he let the man go. It is believed that the man he saw was covered in grease like a mechanic.

From the beheading of Charles one, it is written that the executioners and the assassins will be disguised with face masks and wigs.

But then again, the Beast might have used this to create a diversion. A decoy to confuse the people.

The weapon of execution.

In the execution of Charles I, the axe was the weapon that caused death. The Beast will create a case where the authorities must fake things. They can't say the axe was used in the case of JFK. Recall the Beast is superimposing all three executions into one. So, the bullet that struck JFK must be a magic bullet that doesn't break because this bullet is the same to hit John Connally in several places as well without breaking. All this is symbolic to explain that King Charles I passed words to William Juxon, who wrote the message using shorthand [writing]. You will find out that the bullet is also believed to have hit John Connally as well in the hand [Shot hand].

The magic bullet represents the axe used to behead king Charles I.

The Killer of John F Kennedy: To be resolved likely, Lee Harvey Oswald.

Another easy way to find out who was regarded as responsible for the death of the King and president JFK we simply find out who was exhumed after they had already died.

First Lee Harvey Oswald.

Was Oswald exhumed?

05

Yes exhumed in October 1981.

The body resting in Lee Harvey Oswald's coffin was removed from its grave today, and a team of examining pathologists said that the remains were indeed Oswald's. The finding appeared to end speculation that the corpse might have been that of a Russian agent sent here to kill President Kennedy in 1963.

''We, both individually and as a team, have concluded beyond any doubt, and I mean beyond any doubt, that the individual buried under the name Lee Harvey Oswald in Rose Hill Cemetery is Lee Harvey Oswald,'' said Dr. Linda Norton, head of the team of pathologists who examined the remains today at Baylor University Medical Center here.

https://www.nytimes.com/1981/10/05/us/oswald-s-body-is-exhumed-an-autopsy-affirms-identity.html

Never mind what they say about Lee Harvey Oswald's double as the reason for exhuming the body. The body was exhumed because of the "Bill of attainder". Lee Harvey Oswald had killed the president and, as such, must have a posthumous execution. This included hanging, drawing, beheading, or dissection.

The way for the exhumation was cleared when a temporary restraining order issued by a local judge expired at midnight. Oswald's brother, Robert, who lives in Wichita Falls, had sought in court for some time to block the exhumation.

This is the throwing of the body into the gallows.

After the autopsy, the remains, together with fragments of the wooden coffin, were reburied in a metal coffin and steel vault. [pit and gallows] ---- Needs of Family Cited.

https://www.nytimes.com/1981/10/05/us/oswald-s-body-is-exhumed-an-autopsy-affirms-identity.html

Was Lyndon Johnson exhumed?

Published September 2, 1998

WASHINGTON, DC–Vowing to "restore morality, integrity, and accountability to the office of the presidency," Special Prosecutor Kenneth Starr ordered the exhumation of President Lyndon Johnson's corpse Tuesday in connection with possible sexual misconduct during his tenure in the White House.

The mastermind; the real killer.

The Beast.

The main script to use.

The Execution of the King of England Charles 1 30 January 1649.

The following is what is expected of the President of the US John F. Kennedy on his assassination. He must do exactly what King Charles I did or somehow the Beast, who is the film director, must make sure that the president of the United States John F. Kennedy must do exactly what King Charles I did.

The Setting.

1. The High Court Setting at the time was the same as a modern-day open limousine.

See this link.

https://upload.wikimedia.org/wikipedia/commons/d/da/Court-charles-I-sm.jpg

The platform was draped in black. {Black limousine}

2. Staples had been driven into the wood for ropes to be run through if Charles needed to be restrained. {Seat belt of the limousine would be used if needed}.

3. The execution block was so low that the king would have had to prostrate himself to place his head on the block. {JFK seating in the limousine is already in the prostrate position. Rotating Charles I's position at a right angle (90 degrees) gives us a JFK position. See also book cover.

4. The executioners of Charles were hidden behind face masks and wigs to prevent identification. {This can explain why Lee Harvey Oswald had two Selective Service System identifications with the same face but with two different names: Lee Harvey Oswald and Alek James Hidell.

5. The executioner had an assistant. Accuracy was needed, but the executioner needed someone to guide him if the president was in the correct position. Even though the assistant didn't have a gun, he had something the executioner might look at as a guide if in the correct position. A flag that is raised or an umbrella that can be opened when the president was in the correct position in terms of distance from the position of the executioner. The umbrella man might have had a role to play in guiding the executioner. Recall I said this is a combination of three executions of three leaders. The Beast blended all three into one, so we expect to find all events in the past two assassinations of leaders; the prime minister of Britain and the King of England. The Umbrella man represented the killer of Spencer Perceval, the British Prime Minister, as evidenced by his actions after the shooting. Cool and calculated, I went to sit

down on the pavement. This could only be symbolic, representing John Bellingham after blasting Spencer Perceval twice in the chest. The first shot is to make him raise his hand as a signal, just like what King Charles did. As a signal to let the assassin or execution finish him off.

6. Charles came through the window of the Banqueting Hall. The Beast will make the killer be at the window.

What King Charles I did during his execution.

He protested, claiming that he was innocent, but the heavy security guards meant that even if he raised his voice, the people would not hear his final words. So, he told William Juxon his words. This William Juxon listened to the King's words and used shorthand to write everything he said down.

He borrowed the nightcap [hat] of William Juxon to hold his hair so that the beheading man won't have problems with his long hair.

He told his killer that he will give him a signal with his hand when he was ready to be beheaded.

Charles gave Juxon his George, sash and cloak—uttering one cryptic word: "remember".

He called himself "a martyr of the people"—claiming he would be killed for their rights.

He lay down in a prostrate position (or flat on the ground) because the beheading block was low to the ground and deliberately put that low as a way of showing that the people are the boss and not a tyrannical king. As a way of submitting.

Charles laid his neck out on the block and asked the executioner to wait for his signal to behead him. In a prostrate position with his face and eyes fixed on the ground, the only way to communicate with the executioner is to use his hands as a signal to the executioner that he is ready.

Only a moment passed, and Charles gave the signal and the executioner beheaded him in a clean cut. To behead a person in a prostrate position, the executioner must be on the side top of the person to be headed. The executioner was on his left side, hence the slight tilting to the left.

If the head is beheaded, it hits the ground due to gravity after the beheading. So the Beast will want to include this effect. This is crucial as this will explain why there is confusion as to where he was shot. In the back of the head or from the right front.

The beheading executioner picked up the head of Charles I. The Beast made sure that JFK's wife or secret service played part of the executioner when she or he picked up part of his skull and brain matter removed by the impact of the bullet.

The executioner silently held up Charles' head to the spectators.

The executioner did not utter the customary cry of "Behold the head of a traitor!" either from inexperience or fear of identification.

The executioner dropped the king's head into the crowd and the soldiers swarmed around it.

Dipping their handkerchiefs in his blood and cutting off the locks of his hair. It is believed that the following secret services were covered in JFK's blood and brain matter.

The body was then put in a coffin and covered with black velvet.

His body was placed in the king's former 'lodging chamber' in Whitehall. [

The identities of the executioner of Charles I and his assistant were never revealed to the public, with crude face masks and wigs hiding them at the execution, [46] and they were probably only known to Oliver Cromwell and a few of his colleagues.

So, the Beast will incorporate all the above step by step in the assassination of the President of the United States John F Kennedy as he is using the script of the beheading of King Charles I of England on 30 January 1649.

Let's find out if our hypothesis holds water. Can JFK do exactly what King Charles I did?

JFK must do exactly what is in the script: What King Charles I did during his execution.

He protested, claiming that he was innocent, but the heavy security guards meant that even if he raised his voice, the people would not hear his final words. So, he told William Juxon his words. This William Juxon listened to the King's words and used shorthand to write everything he said down.

A day before he arrived in Dallas on 21 November 1963, JFK was accused by Lyndon Johnson and others through the Wanted for Treason Leaflet of treason against the people who put him in power. On 22 November the first bullet was to symbolize his talking to John Collany playing William Juxon. The bullet through the throat took words out of the king to the body of John Collany through his hand. This is done or used to explain that he wrote down the words of the president using shorthand (Shot hand). This explains why the government came up with the Magic bullet theory. This magic bullet theory explains what happened to this. Recall the Beast must do his best to go by the script of what happened on the execution of Charles I of England. Hence all the arguments by the secret service of the magic bullet.

He borrowed the nightcap [hat] of William Juxon to hold his hair so that the beheading man won't have problems with his long hair.

But to borrow a nightcap of William Juxon played by John Collany, there must be something that must happen. So, the Beast made sure that his brain matter would be all over the place to explain why he needed something to hold his hair, in this case, his head or hair in place.

He told his killer that he will give him a signal with his hand when he was ready to be beheaded.

The need to give a signal explains why all are shot twice. The first bullet is to make prime minister Spencer Perceval and President JFK give a signal. Make them act as if they have given a signal through involuntary hand movements after the first shot. Prime minister was first shot in the chest, making him raise his hand. This is the signal, then the killer John Bellingham fires the fatal shot. In the case of JFK, the first shot through the neck was to make the president give a signal to the killer by raising his hand as he clutched his neck. In the beheading of Charles I, his head was fixed on the block facing down. The King could not see the killer and because of the crowd's noises could not talk or be heard by the executioner. So, he must hand the signal. The shooting in the neck disables word signals so that JFK can only sign through their hands. Another explanation is the fact that since he was found guilty of treason, as explained by the leaflets distributed on 21 November 1963 [Wanted for Treason], he had no right to talk after that. So, lifting the hands involuntarily as a reflex of the first bullet is all the killer wants to perform the execution.

Charles gave Juxon his George, sash and cloak—uttering one cryptic word: "remember". This can explain why the Beast aimed to blast the brain of the President and remove the brain of the president that will stay with either William Juxon played by John

15

Connally. Leaving his brain symbolizes the remembering part.

He called himself "a martyr of the people"—claiming he would be killed for their rights.

JFK might have known his fate. We believed his talks of enemies within were a reference to his hacking possible by the British. Remotely the British might have been torturing him. Hacked the time he lived in England when his father was the ambassador to Britain between 1938 to 1939. We also believe this is also one of the reasons he was assassinated. The US government, the FBI, the CIA, etc. knew he was chipped by the British. Therefore, was a British puppet a traitor to the American people. But what can he do if he complains about the hacking? The people will say he is hallucinating? If he tells the other people, they will call him a traitor and want to get rid of him. If he is to die, he is dying for the people as a martyr, not because of a fault of his own. He and his brother Robert Jr. Kennedy speaking of the enemies within as else. We know too how he met his demise. Even though someone else pulled the trigger, the Beast is the one behind all this.

He lay down in a prostrate position (or flat on the ground) because the beheading block was low to the ground and deliberately put that low as a way of showing that the people are the boss and not a tyrannical king. As a way of submitting.

The Beast must match Charles I prostrate position on his beheading. The Beast, if it rotates right angle anticlockwise Charles I in a prostrate position to 135 degrees, we have JFK's position in the limousine. If the murder weapon was at a right angle above; an axe in Charles I's case. The murder weapon should follow too that it will come from 135 degrees from horizontal. The Texas School Book Depository, especially from that sixth-floor window.

Do you know the Map of London at the time in question if rotated right angle [90 degrees] will match the Dealey Plaza Grassy Knoll Dallas Texas?

This makes the Grassy Knoll where JFK was murdered match the place outside the Banqueting House where King Charles I died.

The Texas School Book Depository corresponds to St James Palace. The place of the queen of Britain at the time of the JFK assassination. During the time of Charles, I, the same part of the palace was part of the library, later turned into a military barracks or place of residence for soldiers.

Charles laid his neck out on the block and asked the executioner to wait for his signal to behead him. In a prostrate position with his face and eyes fixed on the ground, the only way to communicate with the executioner is to use his hands as a signal to the executioner that he is ready.

This can explain the slight tilting to the left where the executioner was standing, even though King Charles I was facing downwards. The executioner had to wait for a signal given by hand.

Only a moment passed, and Charles gave the signal and the executioner beheaded him in a clean cut.

This explains the shot time between bullets. The first bullet is to make the president involuntarily give a signal and the time between the signal and the execution is just a moment. A short time. The Beast to go by the script must train the assassin to be very fast for the first shot to be followed by the second bullet. The killer bullet. This is true in all cases, including the assassination of the British prime minister and the JFK case.

To behead a person in a prostrate position, the executioner must be on the side top of the person to be headed. The executioner was on his left side, hence the slight tilting to the left.

If the head falls to the ground after beheading, it hits the floor. Since the executioner will be on the left side, the head will be slightly tilted to the left and if it falls, it is going to hit the ground opposite the right front side. This explains why some people thought that the bullet was from the front. But knowing how Charles I died and the need for the Beast to follow the script, the fatal bullet came from the back. Any frontal wounds on the forehead are a result of the impact on the ground. But this might make the Beast put two killers. One to fire the fatal shot from the back and one to fire an impact shot from the front right. Grassy Knoll. Note that here, a shot from the Grassy knoll can signify or represent the impact with the ground or floor. As I said, the Beast will do everything it can to match the first script. Just knowing how Charles I was executed explains all the theories and explanations by the officials. All their explanations are explaining the death of a king charged with treason against the people. A huge symbolic event in the history of mankind. That no one is above the law. Even a tyrannical king can fall at the hand of the common man. This is exactly what was happening here. The same thing happened in the assassination of Spencer Perceval by John Bellingham.

If the head is beheaded, it hits the ground due to gravity after the beheading. So, the Beast will want to include this effect. This is crucial as this will explain why there is confusion as to where he was shot. In the back of the head or from the right front. This can explain why all the confusion and different accounts of where JFK was shot. The front or the back. The Beast might have swapped the corpse or given two different corpses to two different hospitals.

In the beheading of Charles I it is written that he had a Doublet;- meaning an inner garment [jacket]. But the Beast might have put two corpses with one as a double of JFK. This could explain all the different autopsy contradicting reports.

The executioner silently held up Charles' head to the spectators. The Beast might have planned all this so that JFK's wife plays the part of the executioner where she lifts part of JFK's head to the people where she crawled on the bonnet to pick up part of JFK's head. We also know the executioner of king Charles I, stood on his left side, the perfect place to behead the head. There are photos of his wife lifting a hand taken from the side just to signify carrying the axe to chop off his head. The one to pick his head as well. But I am not saying that she was involved. The Beast makes it look like that. Also, the secret service man [Clint Hill] standing inside JFK limousine with a leg on the bottom just seconds after being shot signifies the moment just after beheading Charles I. That means the Clint Hill plays the executioner of JFK. This can also point to who was responsible for the death of JFK: the secret service themselves. Recall the need to blast JFK so hard so that his blood ends up all over their clothes and vehicles?

The executioner did not utter the customary cry of "Behold the head of a traitor!" either from inexperience or fear of identification. This can explain why no one claimed that it was them. This can also explain why, even if it was Lee Harvey Oswald who killed the president, he was simply going to deny it. In the assassination of the British prime minister, it can be said that John Bellingham declared that he was the killer symbolizing the shouting; Behold the head of the traitor. But in the JFK assassination, no one accepted responsibility.

The soldiers were covered with the blood of the king as they dipped their handkerchiefs in his blood and cut off the locks of his hair. It is believed that the following secret services were covered in JFK's blood and brain matter. The cutting off of locks can mean his death frees them. They are now free, meaning they might be the ones who had set him up. The ones who have betrayed him. The ones who have got him killed. This is because his death frees their locks. They can't be held accountable for his death, now they had easily killed him in cold blood.

The body was then put in a coffin and covered with black velvet. This will explain the confusion about what coffin JFK was delivered in.

The identities of the executioner of Charles I and his assistant were never revealed to the public, with crude face masks and wigs hiding them at the execution, [46] and they were probably only known to Oliver Cromwell and a few of his colleagues.

The identity of the killer and his assistant were only known by Oliver Cromwell. The one to take over. After all, he is the one who chose them. But does that mean he is the Killer our Beast? Or is he acting on behalf of the people?

Crude face masks and wigs hid the identity of the executioner.

a] Oswald can be regarded as the killer because he had masked his face by the use of two different identities. He had two Selective Service System cards, one in the name of Lee Harvey Oswald and the other with Alek James Hidell.

b] Since this is a combination of three events in high treason cases. The other executioner is JFK's wife. This scene is representing the axe-holding executioner who beheaded King Charles I simply because of the position she was in. Her act of being made to pick up part of his head and the crude face [make-up] and wigs the wool hat she was wearing. Again, I reiterate here just as a symbol.

Oliver Cromwell played by Lyndon Johnson.

After the First English Civil War, the parliamentarians accepted the premise that the King, although wrong, had been able to justify his fight, and that he would still be entitled to limited powers as

King under a new constitutional settlement. By provoking the Second English Civil War even while defeated and in captivity, Charles was held responsible for unjustifiable bloodshed. The secret "Engagement" treaty with the Scots was considered particularly unpardonable; "a more prodigious treason", said Oliver Cromwell, "than any that had been perfected before; because the former quarrel was that Englishmen might rule over one another; this to visualize us to a foreign nation." [1] Cromwell, up to this point, had supported negotiations with the king but now rejected further negotiations.

[The secret "Engagement" treaty with the Scots was considered particularly unpardonable; "a more prodigious treason", said Oliver Cromwell, "than any that had been perfected before; because the former quarrel was that Englishmen might rule over one another; this to visualise us to a foreign nation.".

This is the support for the argument that JFK might have been hacked as a kid by the British who listened to all he did. Hence others saw him as just a puppet of the British. One to sell their freedoms to a foreign government.]

In making war against Parliament, the king had caused the deaths of thousands. Estimated deaths from the first two English civil wars have been reported as 84,830 killed, with estimates of another 100,000 dying from the war-related disease.

Following the second civil war, the New Model Army and the Independents in Parliament determined that the King should be punished.

He is probably the only one who knew the executioners. I can only assume that he is the one who had chosen and picked these. So, as such, the person behind the assassination. But might be following the commands of the Beast.

The common execution of Richard Brandon and his father Gregory

Brandon.

There are strong beliefs that Richard Brandon, the executioner of the time, was the one who killed Charles I. Some attribute the beheading to his father, Gregory Brandon.

Lee Harvey Oswald, when asked where he was at the time of the shooting of JFK, suggested that he was with Junior and the other one. During the assassination of Charles I, Richard Brandon was known as young Gregory or junior. If it is not him who killed the king, the Beast put him also at the scene of a murder.

The Precedence of killing a King and A prime minister. [Oswald photos CE133A and CE133B]

Explanations of Lee Harvey Oswald's photos holding a gun in the backyard.

Commission Exhibit CE 133A, CE133B and CE133C

https://www.history-matters.com/archive/jfk/wc/wcvols/wh16/html/WH_Vol16_0267b.htm

The three photos are the result of the Beast who is using these to explain the precedents of a high treason assassination. To recap, I said the JFK assassination is a combination of three events all in one. This assassination will have elements of the Execution of Charles 1 of England on 30 January 1649. Secondly will include all elements of the assassination of British Prime Minister Spencer Perceval on 11 May 1812 and the JFK assassination itself.

Check the above link for the photos from the Warren Commission documents.

Analysis of Commission Exhibit photo C133A.

This is the precedence of killing king Charles 1 for high treason against the people. The weapon that caused the death came from the left side where the executioner was standing. The axe came from the left side.

Analysis of the Commission Exhibit 133B photo of Lee Harvey Oswald.

This represents the assassination of British Prime Minister Spencer Perceval on 11 May 1812.

The British prime minister, after committing high treason, was blasted in the chest with two bullets by John Bellingham. Photo 133B explains the direction of the bullets that killed the victim. The two newspapers Oswald is holding represent the bullets or the two counts of treason and tyranny. Oswald in this photo changes the hand holding the gun, signifying a change of weapon.

Analysis of the Commission Exhibit 133C Oswald's photo holding the gun over his head.

This photo is believed to have been burned at the command of Lee Oswald's mother. It is said that Oswald had the gun raised over his head. This explains the event that was going to happen. The bullets now we're going to come from overhead, the Texas School Book Depository. The weapon will be high up.

At first, the weapon came from the side in Charles I 's beheading. Secondly, in the assassination of Spencer Perceval, the shots came from the front. Now the bullets will come from over the head high from the sixth floor of the Texas Book Depository.

This can also mean that first in Charles I, the local people are the ones who ordered the execution. The second can refer to execution from a peer in the case of John Bellingham, but now [then] the judgment will come from afar and from someone above too. This can signify commands from another monarchy, or power from abroad.

2

The Predictability of the Beast.

I argued throughout my books that the Beast simply goes back in history and gets scripts from there and uses these to trigger all kinds of crimes.

The Beast follows a predictable method. In all cases, it hacks or chips people from birth and grooms them throughout life. Making them pose for photos, they want photos that match drawings from as far as the 1200s or 1600s.

It then asks the people to stand for a photo or photos to match the ones from the script it is using or to explain what is going to happen.

In most cases, the photos are to implicate the subjects and exonerate themselves.

The photos in this case are to represent the two situations where a leader has been killed by the common people for high treason and tyranny.

Tyburn tree is represented by the triple underpass in Dealey Plaza in Dallas, Texas.

Tyburn Tree was the site of public hangings, possibly established as early as 1108. The first recorded execution was in 1196. In 1571, a wooden scaffold was erected in a triangular shape, able to host three hangings simultaneously, perfect for a waiting crowd eager for some entertainment.

https://lookup.london/tyburn-tree-hidden-history-marble-arch/

Public hangings were very popular.

The importance of this Tyburn represented by the triple underpass [meaning a place where the souls go to the underworld] is the fact that Oliver Cromwell the one who lead the execution of the King of England Charles I was later posthumously executed here following his exhumation from where he was buried at Westminster Abbey on 30 January 1661 on the same day as the king but twelve years later.

This can indicate who might have been thought to be the mastermind of the King's death. This is because the King's son had taken over to avenge his father's death. The regicides: the king's killer must face the same fate. The fact that he was posthumously executed on the same day 30 January, but twelve years later, might hint at that.

A number of the 59 regicides of Charles I of England, including the most prominent of the regicides, the former Lord Protector Oliver Cromwell, died before the Restoration of his son Charles II in 1660. Parliament passed an order of attainder for High Treason on the four most prominent deceased regicides: John Bradshaw, the court president; Oliver Cromwell; Henry Ireton; and Thomas Pride. [10] The bodies were exhumed and three were hanged for a day at Tyburn and then beheaded. The three bodies were then thrown into a pit close to the gallows, while the heads were placed, with Bradshaw's in the middle, at the end of Westminster Hall (the symbolism was lost on no one as that was the building where the trial of Charles I had taken place).

Wikipedia.

https://en.wikipedia.org/wiki/Posthumous_execution

Although deceased by the time of the Restoration, the regicides John Bradshaw, Oliver Cromwell, Henry Ireton, and Thomas

Pride were served with a bill of attainder on 15 May 1660 backdated to 1 January 1649 (NS). After the committee stages, the bill passed both the Houses of Lords and Commons and was engrossed on 4 December 1660. This was followed by a resolution that passed both Houses on the same day:[29][30][31]

That the carcasses of Oliver Cromwell, Henry Ireton, John Bradshaw, and Thomas Pride, whether buried in Westminster Abbey, or elsewhere, be, with all Expedition, taken up, and drawn upon a Hurdle to Tyburn, and there hanged up in their Coffins for some time; and after that buried under the said Gallows: And that James Norfolk Esquire, Sergeant at Arms attending the House of Commons, do take care that this Order is put ineffectual Execution.

Wikipedia.

https://en.wikipedia.org/wiki/Bill_of_attainder

The Bill of Attainder points to those who were thought to have caused the death of the king.

The judges in all 3 cases

John Bradshaw versus King Charles I

Sir James Mansfield versus John Bellingham

Jack Ruby versus Lee Harvey Oswald.

John Bradshaw was the judge of the High Court of Justice. The one who sentenced the king to be beheaded.

59 regicides signed the death warrant of king Charles I.

The Beast had at least 59 people who colluded to get the president killed, just as those who got the king of England killed, but the number of all the people who were involved was as high as 104.

Twenty-four of these people had already died by the time the King's son took over in 1660 at the restoration.

Four notorious ones were given posthumous execution.

The bodies were exhumed, hanged, and beheaded. Then their bodies were cast in a pit into the gallows. The heads of the four notorious ones were put on spikes and placed outside Westminster Hall. Those who were still alive were hanged, drawn, and quartered. 19 were imprisoned for life.

The property was confiscated by many, and most were barred from holding public office or title again. Twenty-one of those under threat fled England, mostly settling in the Netherlands or Switzerland; three settled in New England.

Wikipedia.

It must be noted that the list was just a blacklist, meaning some of the people on the list might have been innocent. The trial of King Charles I consisted of 135 commissioners.

3

Executive Summary

Superimposing three high treason cases in the history of mankind all in one on 22 November 1963.

Superimposing three cases of beheading

King Charles 1 of England 30 January 1649,

The assassination of Prime Minister Spencer Perceval on 11 May 1812

The assassination of President John Frederick Kennedy on 22 November 1963.

Crimes of the King of England, the Prime Minister of Britain, and the President of the United States.

High Treason

High Tyranny

What happened on 22 November 1963 was a combination of the two cases where a king or prime minister was executed and assassinated for high treason committed against the people. Normally, high treason is a crime against the crown or prime minister. But what if it's the king, prime minister, and president committing crimes against its people?

What are the crimes of these three leaders? King Charles 1, Prime Minister Spencer Perceval, and President JFK.

High Treason and High Tyranny.

Charles I, believed in the divine rights of kings, meaning that he believed that he was appointed by God and only God could overrule him.

King Charles married a catholic, something that offended the English protestants.

Charles I, wanted to rule alone without a parliament, so he continuously dissolved parliament only to assemble it when he needed money. Parliament would collect taxes and fund the King.

He engaged in expensive foreign wars, sacrificing the soldiers.

He neglected public welfare issues.

This man is wanted for treasonous activities against the United States.

It was Prime Minister Spencer Perceval's pleasure that justice should not be granted.

Trampling on the law and right in the belief that no retribution could reach him.

Prime Minister Spencer sets himself above the law, something he does at his risk, hence the assassination or execution.

The prime minister acted wrong, disregarding the birth rights of its people. After all, these people were not demanding favor, no. But for their rights to be upheld.

JFK was accused of putting personal goals first before people and country.

JFK is accused of embarking on wars that bring harm to the people, hence his acts are contrary to the public interests as his actions were bringing harm to the people hence the treason charges.

Betraying the constitution, which he swore to uphold. He is turning the sovereignty of the US over to the communist-controlled United Nations.

He is betraying our friends Cuba, Katanga, and Portugal and befriending our enemies (Russia, Yugoslavia, Poland.)

He has been wrong on innumerable issues affecting the security of the US (United Nations -Berlin wall - missile removal - Cuba wheat deals - Tes Ban treaty, etc.)

He has been lax in enforcing communist registration laws.

He has given support and encouragement to the communist-inspired racial riots.

He has illegally invaded a sovereign state with federal troops.

He has consistently appointed anti-Christians to federal office; upholds the supreme court in its anti-Christian rulings. Aliens and now communists abound in federal office.

He has been caught in fantastic lies to the American people (including personal ones like his previous marriage and divorce.)

[Wanted for Treason leaflet 21November 1963]

Setting

The High Court of Justice for the trial at the time of Charles I, King of England, resembles the open JFK limousine.

The Executing Scaffold.

Outside the Banqueting House during Charles I 1649 [England] outside Grassy Knoll in Dealey Plaza [United States. Rotate the maps ant-clockwise 90 degrees]

4

To find out who killed President John Frederick Kennedy JFK, we propose a working hypothesis. A precedent we have on records and assuming that if the same crime is to happen again, then it must follow the same stencil. The script and the blueprint of the murder of someone as important as a president.

We as Tomorrow's World Order and as the First Global President have discovered that every event that has occurred in life is a matter of history repeating itself.

I know it sounds unbelievable, but trusts me.

I believe every bad or good event can be explained by another event in the past. We have precedents of all events that occurred in the last centuries. We have concluded that some countries are just repeating history. They are just going into the past and recreating a past event just like then, in some cases, using paintings to find the actors or people then who look exactly like people as far back as in the 1660s.

I know right now you are rubbing all this off as nonsense. But hold that thought. Nonsense to who? To you because you are the reader and there are no benefits to you.

But think about the people who benefit from all this.

I tell you the ability to predict the future is every man's dream, especially among power-mad lunatics. People who want to control the world. To these people, the ability to determine everyone's future is a driving force so powerful that they recreate events that no one else knows about. Events they have documented over centuries and events they can recreate and know exactly how things will unfold. All this is to have a competitive advantage over everyone else.

The ability to act as problem solvers for others even if this means killing thousands, etc.

For argument's sake, we will call these people, governments, culprits, etc the Beast from now on.

Another assumption is that the Beast believes is a great problem solver and will help anyone in any government that is in difficulties by prescribing a solution from the past. The Beast believes that any problem has been felt throughout history. The assumption is that history repeats itself. So, whatever a country is experiencing right now they have already gone through that situation in the past, often centuries ago.

So, what the Beast does is simply go back to the past and look for a similar situation and prescribe an event to solve that problem. So, the Beast is like a doctor. Just look at the problems, check the symptoms and causes and prescribe a solution to solve this.

So, the working idea is that everything that is happening now has a precedent already.

But the Beast is deceptive and malicious in that it might set up someone to cover its tracks so that people might not know exactly what is happening.

Every event has a blueprint; a script; a masterpiece drawn and drafted and documented but only a few can suspect and know about this.

Every event must follow exactly the scripts of the reference event for the same outcome to be achieved.

But the objectives and aims of the event might be different from that of the original event.

Whoever is behind this might use malicious deception in prescribing this event as a solution to a current issue but with other personal motives.

Above all the Beast prescribes solutions to gain from all this but not necessarily in terms of money no.

i]The Beast does this to gain competitively and monetarily.

ii] The beast does this to gain the trust of the people it helps.

iii] The Beast does this to show power and who is the boss.

iv] The Beast does this to determine the course of history.

v] The Beast does this to deal with problem-people, mainly presidents.

vi] The Beast does this to impose protectorate protection where it imposes its service, especially to presidents who are in difficult situations but to corner them and hold them hostage. A perfect example is when the Beast kills a person or people themselves where it benefits the president and where all the evidence points to the president as having a hand in the killings. Then blackmail the president; asking for favor and threatening to set up the president as the evidence points to the president. Then go on to go after all the people who accuse the president and blame the president for the killings. Then brag to protect the president by eliminating all the trouble caused. In this case, the president has nothing to do with the killings, but all the evidence points to him as the culprit.

Our Working Hypothesis.

I have pointed out that every event is explained by another event in the past that acts as a precedent. The script, and blueprint of that event is that to understand any event no matter how horrific the event was there is an explanation for that. That means every event is just a repeat of an event in the past.

Note that here it doesn't matter if the event happened by chance or not. We will look at that later.

The Logic.

So, to find out why a current event has happened we use logic and do reverse engineering. Meaning going back to the past to look for answers.

The reason is that the event happened as it happened in the past. So to know why it happened and who did it we simply visit the past and rearrange actors, people events, etc. to match that of the past and when that does not correspond then we know that something is wrong.

Pre-test of our hypothesis.

But first, before I look at the JFK assassination, we need to test our hypothesis and see if it holds water. We look at the current major events of our days. The Russia and Ukraine war.

To understand our hypothesis, the reader is requested to read our Russia and Ukraine War/Special Military Prediction.

https://play.google.com/store/books/details/David_Gomadza_A_Pe

rfect_Prediction_Russia_Ukraine?id=PmaVEAAAQBAJ&gl=GB
&pli=1

We used our hypothesis to find why this war occurred by visiting similar events and we indeed found a match. The Second Anglo-Dutch War of 1665-1667 was a perfect match.

The same issues then have arisen. Remember our working hypothesis that history repeats itself. The British to gain a competitive advantage and dominate the grain trade in the 1660s triggered the Second Anglo-Dutch war.

The rest is history.

Check the astonishing accuracy of our Russia and Ukraine War Prediction day by day and event by event.

We believe that the West, the UK and the US will escalate the war by providing weapons and giving Ukraine a sense of hope that they can defeat a nuclear weapon state by July 2024 just before presidential elections in the UK and US in 2024.

We are not judging but we will give our perspective at the end.

We encourage you the reader to download our war prediction for free and read it first then come back to Tomorrow's World Order's perspective on the JFK assassination.

Once done fasten your seat belts because this is a nerve-wracking roller-coaster.

Warning not for the fainthearted. Get your panic attack bags.

We believe the assassination of the President of the United States on 22 November 1963 was an event that was modeled on two scripts.

The assassination of British Prime Minister Spencer Perceval by

John Bellingham on 11 May 1812 at 5.15 pm.

The execution of Charles I the king of England on 30 January 1649.

If we are correct, it follows too that whatever happened on this day and all the actors must fit those of these two events.

But we also believe that since there are two events interwoven together, it can be that one is a cover for the other to misdirect the people and create a conspiracy so that whoever did this will never be caught.

So outright we believe our culprit is a person, cult, government agents, etc who are familiar with these two events and who triggered the assassination of JFK with the help of the Beast.

5

First working hypothesis. The assassination of Spencer Perceval on 11 May 1812.

The assassination of the President of the United States must fit the assassination of Spencer Perceval.

The assassin of JFK must fit John Bellingham.

He must be put through the same ordeal as John Bellingham.

The circumstances must match.

The motive to kill must match or be related.

Other factors must be the same as well.

The Script.

The actors.

John Bellingham played by Lee Harvey Oswald.

Prime Minister Spencer Perceval was played by President John Frederick Kennedy.

Judge Sir James Mansfield played by Jack Ruby.

Maria Bellingham is played by Marina Oswald.

Jane Perceval played by Jacqueline Kennedy Onassis.

Isaac Gascoyne is played by Roy Truly.

Critical factors.

The inability of insurance companies or the government to pay for compensation, unemployment benefits insurance, or redress of some sort and all this due to suspected forgery or fraud as the trigger of what follows.

We can only infer that Oswald could have been denied compensation, benefits, and insurance through the Selective Service System. The reason that Oswald had two identities in different names meant denial of any benefits. The FBI might have set him up tricking him to act as an informant in the Fair Play for Cuba Committee. So that they caught him red-handed with two IDS hence easy for them to deny any help he is entitled to. The FBI pestered his wife due to his fraud or forgery of documents using the Espionage Act as a cover to drive him mad. A man who can't afford to help his wife who has just had a baby. This is a trigger to drive him mad and target JFK who might have made the claiming process hard.

It could be claims of being imprisoned whilst still in the army in the US. Or it could have been abuse suffered in Russia.

Not sure how bad it was in Russia. The question to ask is how bad the situation was then. Okay enough to drive him to come back. But Marina could have simply agreed to marry him simply because she gets US citizenship as well and therefore encouraged him to come back.

Could the treatment in Russia have been so bad as to smoke JFK?

Any man in John Bellingham's shoes would blast anyone president, prime minister, etc. Oswald got a wife and a baby from Russia. Not sure this can be bad enough to kill the president.

Critical factors related to John Bellingham must be matched by the killer of the President of the United States for our hypothesis to hold water.

John Bellingham

Bellingham's early life is largely unknown, and most post-assassination biographies included speculation as fact. Recollections of family and friends show that Bellingham was born in St Neots, Huntingdonshire,[1] and brought up in London, where he was apprenticed to a jeweler, James Love, aged fourteen. Two years later, he went as a midshipman on the maiden voyage of the Hartwell from Gravesend to China. A mutiny took place on 22 May 1787, which led to the ship running aground and sinking (off the coast of Africa).

In autumn 1803, the Russian ship Soleure [2] (or sometimes "Sojus"), insured at Lloyd's of London, had been lost in the White Sea. Her owners (the house of R. Van Brienen) filed a claim on their insurance, but an anonymous letter told Lloyd the ship had been sabotaged. Soloman Van Brienen believed Bellingham was the author, and retaliated by accusing him of a debt of 4,890 roubles to the bankruptcy of which he was an assignee.[clarification needed] Bellingham, about to return from Russia to Britain on 16 November 1804, had his traveling pass withdrawn because of the alleged debt.

Wikipedia.

He went to Russia, Arkhangelsk.

He was an unsuccessful businessman who developed grievances with the government for their failure to help him when he was imprisoned in Russia.

He spent years in jail for debt from 1804 despite contacting the government to rescue him; they all ignored him spending more than five years in a Russian jail.

His grievances were the lack of support from the government and he also blamed it for his financial difficulties.

He petitioned the government; the prime minister Spencer Perceval all with limited success.

He started petitioning the government for compensation for his imprisonment, but all this was denied.

Things got worse that he felt the need to be compensated and as this fell on deaf ears the more agitated and frustrated, he became; enough to blast the prime minister.

He believed that he was doing the right thing hence his surprise at the guilty verdict that he remained dumb folded.

He confessed to having experienced all the bad misfortunes any man can experience and that his pains were so huge that the only redress was to blast Spencer Perceval, mainly the ambassador to Russia at the time of his troubles.

Someone must have used all avenues of redress with no luck that he directly warns the authorities that if they don't respond he will be forced to take the law into his own hands with them taking him for a fool until that day.

He would have bought not just one gun but two to kill in case one fails he will have a backup.

Lying in wait. He would have frequented the place he was to carry out the killing to increase the chances of this happening without raising any suspicion. John Bellingham had frequented the House of Commons where he committed the murder. Lee Harvey Oswald worked at the school depository which would increase his chances of blasting JFK without being caught.

He must have been so bent on revenge that he kind of gloated after the killing that he won't run away because he believes that justice had been done and is innocent so no need to escape. He is the equalizer and justice has been done. So appears relaxed and composed.

Will strongly considers himself innocent and he can face any court.

Will deny any claims of insanity because how can he be insane after all he was wronged and all he is doing is correcting a wrong.

All this is to set a point that even the President or Prime Minister is under the law. No wish of a leader can be allowed to become law. Otherwise, if that happens then it means erasing hard-earned liberties.

He might have been tricked by the government agents e.g. in the case of Bellingham he could have been encouraged by the British ambassador to Russia to claim compensation from the Russian government after his initial release which made the situation worse that they put him back in prison. If the ambassador had told him correctly that any claims against the Russian government will see him put back in jail surely, he might have just left Russia after the first year in prison. So, this might be the bitter reason. In Oswald, we can infer that the FBI knew he had no job and on a $33 unemployment pay-out tricked him to make another forged Selective Service System card that fortified any claims to compensation, insurance, or benefits he had with his original card. So, the feeling of being cheated can make him take drastic measures. His reply when asked about Alek James Hidell can explain this when he replied that why should they ask him when they know about this Alek James Hidell. Something he did as they suggested. Could explain why he blasted JFK in the throat as a sign to silence a liar or tricking person. The bullet to the head blows the clever manipulating brain tricking people.

Once home, Bellingham began petitioning the United Kingdom's government for compensation for his imprisonment. This was refused, as the United Kingdom had broken off diplomatic relations with Russia in November 1808. Bellingham's wife urged him to drop the matter, and he did so reluctantly.

Wikipedia.

In 1812, Bellingham renewed his attempts to win compensation. On 18 April, he visited the Foreign Office where a civil servant told him he was at liberty to take whatever measures he thought proper.

On 20 April, Bellingham purchased two .50 caliber (12.7 mm) pistols from a gunsmith at 58 Skinner Street.

He also had a tailor sew an inside pocket to his coat. At this time, he was often seen in the lobby of the House of Commons.

He was often seen in the lobby of the House of Commons where he petitioned the government.

After taking a friend's family to a painting exhibition on 11 May 1812, Bellingham remarked that he had some business to attend to. He made his way to Parliament, where he waited in the lobby.

When Prime Minister Spencer Perceval appeared, Bellingham stepped forward and shot him in the heart.

He then calmly sat on a bench.

He was identified by Isaac Gascoyne who had previously seen him. He was restrained.

After exhausting all avenues of redress to no avail he took the law into his own hands and bought two guns.

On 11 May 1812, he waited for the Prime minister and shot him twice in the chest in the House of the Commons.

Four days later he was put on trial and found guilty and hanged three days later.

Point to note.

6

John Bellingham's Motive.

The motive was Bellingham's groundless claim that the Crown owed him money for time he had served in a Russian prison while Perceval had been Chancellor of the Exchequer."

John Bellingham was tried on Friday 15 May 1812 at the Old Bailey, where he argued that he would have preferred to shoot the British ambassador to Russia, but insisted as a wronged man he was justified in killing the representative of his oppressors.

Wikipedia.

His remarks at the trial.

He made a formal statement to the court, saying:[3]

Recollect, Gentlemen, what was my situation? Recollect that my family was ruined, and myself destroyed, merely because it was Mr. Perceval's pleasure that justice should not be granted; sheltering himself behind the imagined security of his station, and trampling upon law and right in the belief that no retribution could reach him. I demand only my right, and not a favor; I demand what is the birth right and privilege of every Englishman.

Gentlemen, when a minister sets himself above the laws, as Mr. Perceval did, he does it at his [own] risk. If this were not so, the mere will of the minister would become the law, and what would then become of your liberties?

I trust that this serious lesson will operate as a warning to all future ministers and that they will henceforth do the right thing, for if the upper ranks of society are permitted to act wrong with impunity, the inferior ramifications will soon become wholly corrupted.

Gentlemen, my life is in your hands, I rely confidently upon your justice.

Wikipedia.

Points to note here.

He argued that his family was ruined.

His life was destroyed by time lost in prison.

He believed the prime minister denied him justice simply because he can.

He believed that the prime minister thought he was above the law and ignored his pleas simply because he felt invincible and that nothing will befall him. The reason why he trampled upon the law.

What John Bellingham was after was not a favor but his right as a citizen to be listened to and helped when he needed such help.

The problem with the government is believing that they are above the law.

But this was a reminder that such thinking can only be at that Prime Minister's risk as no one is above the law.

He believed that some actions were needed to keep the rule of the law otherwise the prime minister becomes the law. To detect and do as he please which is wrong. In other words, what happened is the result of the Prime Minister's actions. You sow the wind; you can only reap the whirlwind.

In case the Prime Minister's actions, deeds, etc are permitted this can only mean the stripping of hard-earned liberties. Something John Bellingham was against setting up the collision course as imminent and inevitable. Justice will be served.

After all, he believed that this was a birth right and privilege of every Englishman.

John Bellingham is a check in the system to make sure that the prime Ministers won't become the law. To safeguard justice and fair dealings as a warning to future ministers.

He believed that 'for if the upper ranks of society are permitted to act wrong with impunity, the inferior ramifications will soon become wholly corrupted.'

Evidence was presented that Bellingham was insane, but it was discounted by the trial judge, Sir James Mansfield. Bellingham was found guilty and was sentenced to death. [3]

The crowd on his execution believed that he had served his duty:

"You have rendered an important service to your country, you have taught ministers that they should do justice, and grant the audience when it is asked of them. Wikipedia.[4]

Point to note here.

John Bellingham blasted the prime minister twice in the chest as a duty to the country which means doing his duty.

Teaching future ministers and reminding them that they are there to serve the people. That means listening to the people.

This can help us infer who might have triggered all this as a duty to the country, the very fact also that will point to the cover-ups.

Isaac Gascoyne.

Isaac Gascoyne (21 August 1763[1] – 26 August 1841) was a British Army officer and Tory politician. He was born at Barking, London Essex on 21 August 1763.

He was a British Army Officer with the rank of Ensign.

The junior officer in an infantry regiment was traditionally the carrier of the ensign flag.

It was the duty of officers of this rank to carry the color of the regiment. Wikipedia.

In 1796, Gascoyne was elected as a Member of Parliament for Liverpool, succeeding his elder brother, Bamber Gascoyne. [5] While there, he used his position to strongly oppose the abolition of the Slave Trade [6] and the Reform Act of 1832. He also opposed both the abolition of bull-baiting and Catholic Emancipation.

In 1811, Gascoyne received several petitions from Liverpool resident John Bellingham, calling for him to take up his claim for compensation from the British government for a period of imprisonment he had suffered in Russia. In May 1812, Bellingham entered the lobby of the House of Commons and shot Prime Minister Spencer Perceval dead. Gascoyne was able to recognize Bellingham, providing leads in the immediate aftermath. [7][8]

Wikipedia.

Recap of critical events.

In 1803 Bellingham traveled to Russia and on his return journey, a ship called the Soluere had sunk in the White Sea.

This ship was insured by Lloyds of London who suspected fraud after a tip-off and therefore was refusing to pay the insurance claim.

The owner of the ship believed that John Bellingham was the man who had tipped them off to get even apportioned debt to John Bellingham too.

When existing in Russia John Bellingham was arrested for the debt apportioned to him and put in jail.

He sought help pleading his innocence to the British Ambassador in Russia, Lord Granville Leverson Gower

John Bellingham spent two years in a rat-infested prison being fed bread and water because Lord Granville on behalf of the British government had denied interfering.

In his absence, his business fell into difficulties, and he soon had creditors demanding money. One Russian merchant demanded 2,000 rubles owed to him. Bellingham indicated he was unable to pay.

Even though the original allegations against Bellingham had by then been dropped, he was kept in custody - this time as a bankrupt.

Wikipedia.

When the government refused to help John Bellingham remained in jail for six years and when he came out, he was a man bent on revenge or compensation for he believed the government was responsible for the failure of his business and what had befallen him.

If they had helped, he could have come out early to put his business in order.

After leaving Russia he set out to seek compensation from the government by making representations of his case. He had contacted prime minister Spencer Perceval who denied the claim stating that he had no grounds for compensation.

His grievances were that the government had abandoned him to rot in a Russian jail when they could have come to the rescue and as such, he wanted remunerations.

Another critical factor is the fact that his presence did not raise any suspicion because he was well known by then after petitioning ministers to have his case heard.

Bellingham's presence in the House of Commons lobby on 11 May caused no particular suspicion; he had made several recent visits, sometimes asking journalists to confirm specific ministers' identities.

Wikipedia.

The moment Spencer Perceval entered the House of the Commons John Bellingham withdrew the pistol and fired two shots into his chest.

As Perceval entered the lobby, he was confronted by Bellingham who, drawing a pistol, shot the prime minister in the chest. Perceval staggered forward a few steps and exclaimed, "I am murdered!" before falling face down at the feet of William Smith, the MP for Norwich.

Point to note.

John Bellingham's composure.

He was so calm that after blasting the prime minister he sat down on a bench. This is attributed to people who feel wronged and have taken the law into their own hands and carried out what they believe is justice.

If he had walked out quietly, he could have escaped without being known.

Had Bellingham "walked quietly out into the street, he would have escaped, and the committer of the murder would never have been known."

Wikipedia.

John Bellingham admitted the killing of the prime minister, but he believed that he was testifying an injustice and therefore vindicated and justified.

No one was above the law, not even the prime minister. After all, what had happened was a direct result of the Prime Minister's actions.

John Bellingham explained that.

"I have been ill-treated ... I have sought redress in vain. I am a most unfortunate man and feel here"—placing a hand on heart— "sufficient justification for what I have done."

Wikipedia.

I believe due to his continued petitions and demands for compensation the authorities were tired of him and told him off to go and do whatever he wanted for as far as they were concerned he did not qualify for the compensation.

He had, he said, exhausted all proper avenues and had made it clear to the authorities that he proposed to take independent action. He had been told to do his worst:

"I have obeyed them. I have done my worst, and I rejoice in the deed."

7

The political climate at the time.

Discontent with the government and Spencer Perceval's controversial policies meant high alertness. The authorities feared an insurrection.

His assassination by John Bellingham increased those fears that security was tight.

This also explained why his trial was swiftly carried out as he was believed to be part of a conspiracy that required urgent attention.

Even though there were increased fears of an insurrection, an uprising, and that he was part of a conspiracy to overthrow the government. John Bellingham was a one-man assassin with a grudge against the government for the ill-treatment he suffered in Russia.

That means he acted alone.

Despite initial fears that the assassination might be linked to a general uprising, it transpired that Bellingham had acted alone, protesting against the government's failure to compensate him for his treatment a few years previously when he had been imprisoned in Russia for a trading debt.

Wikipedia.

https://en.wikipedia.org/wiki/Assassination_of_Spencer_Perceval

The trial found out that John Bellingham had acted alone.

The court accepted his claim that he had acted alone.

Bellingham's lack of remorse, and apparent certainty that his action was justified, raised questions about his sanity, but at his trial, he was judged to be legally responsible for his actions.

John Bellingham's formal statement to the court.

Recollect, Gentlemen, what was my situation? Recollect that my family was ruined, and myself destroyed, merely because it was Mr. Perceval's pleasure that justice should not be granted; sheltering himself behind the imagined security of his station, and trampling upon law and right in the belief that no retribution could reach him. I demand only my right. Large crowds gathered outside Newgate Prison on 18 May; a force of troops stood by since warnings had been received of a "Rescue Bellingham" movement and not a favor; I demand what is the birth right and privilege of every Englishman.

Gentlemen, when a minister sets himself above the laws, as Mr. Perceval did, he does it at his [own] risk. If this were not so, the mere will of the minister would become the law, and what would then become of your liberties?

I trust that this serious lesson will operate as a warning to all future ministers and that they will henceforth do the right thing, for if the upper ranks of society are permitted to act wrong with impunity, the inferior ramifications will soon become wholly corrupted.

Gentlemen, my life is in your hands, I rely confidently upon your justice.

Wikipedia.

John Bellingham's fate.

He was hanged at Newgate Prison on 18 May, one week after the assassination and one month before the start of the War of 1812.

One critical point to note here is the War of 1812 the United States V United Kingdom.

The War of 1812 (18 June 1812 – 17 February 1815) was fought by the United States of America and its indigenous allies against the United Kingdom and its allies in British North America, with limited participation by Spain in Florida. It began when the United States declared war on 18 June 1812 and, although peace terms were agreed upon in the December 1814 Treaty of Ghent, did not officially end until the peace treaty was ratified by Congress on 17 February 1815. [16][17]

This event is critical and points also to the people behind the assassination of JFK as I will elaborate on later. This is based on our hypothesis that the event to follow follows a script. If they used a precedent that resulted in the war between the USA and the UK. Then it follows too that the intended intention of the assassination of JFK was to trigger fighting between the USA and the UK.

It can be speculated that either the UK assassinated JFK as a challenge to war. Expecting the USA to fight them.

It can also mean that whoever did this wanted the US to trigger a fight with the UK.

Keep this in mind when we look at the assassination of JFK.

A quick look at Spencer Perceval and the political and economic climate at the time.

Perceval's politics were highly conservative, and he acquired a reputation for his attacks on radicalism.

Perceval's government was faced with great political unrest and a low point in the war with Napoleon.

At the outset of his ministry, Perceval enjoyed the strong support of King George III, but in October 1810 the king lapsed into insanity and was permanently incapacitated.

Wikipedia.

Napoleon introduced the Continental system that was meant to destroy Britain's overseas trade.

The Orders permitted the Royal Navy to detain any ship thought to be carrying goods to France or its continental allies. With both warring powers employing similar strategies, world trade shrank, leading to widespread hardship and dissatisfaction in key British industries, particularly textiles and cotton. [18] There were frequent calls for modification or repeal of the Orders,[19] which damaged relations with the United States to the point that, by early 1812, the two nations were on the brink of war. [18][20]

Wikipedia.

Spencer Perceval maintained his reputation of being strict with radicals. He had imprisoned Burdett and William Cobbett.

The radical MP Sir Francis Burdett was committed to the Tower of London for having published a letter in William Cobbett's Political Register denouncing the government's exclusion of the press from the inquiry.

Perceval had led the Tory government since 1809, during a critical phase of the Napoleonic Wars. His determination to prosecute the war using the harshest of measures caused widespread poverty and unrest on the home front; thus, the news of his death was a cause of rejoicing in the worst-affected parts of the country.

After Perceval's death, Parliament made generous provisions to his widow and children and approved the erection of monuments. Thereafter his ministry was soon forgotten, his policies reversed, and he is generally better known for the manner of his death than for any of his achievements.

The government after Spencer Perceval's death indirectly believed that he was wrong in his policies which most were reversed.

To keep his wife and family from complaining the then-parliament generously compensated them tenfold for what they were expecting.

The government believed Perceval's policies were wrong even though John Bellingham had nevertheless been found guilty; this is something that had to be done. Believing that the prime minister was taking the wrong road.

Point to note here about Prime Minister Spencer Perceval.

Note here that John Bellingham's grievances were the ambassador to Russia.

The big question to address earlier in the analysis is to identify any links between President JFK and Britain or England. A background check shows that he lived in England as a boy when his father was the ambassador to Britain.

John F. Kennedy.

The father of JFK was once an ambassador to Britain, and he wanted to keep America out of the war with Nazi Germany.

During his tumultuous time in London, Joseph Kennedy fought bitterly with the State Department, as well as FDR, in his outspoken opposition to the president's policy of coming to the aid of Britain in the wake of Adolf Hitler's European onslaught.

 Kennedy ruffled feathers in Washington when he met secretly with German diplomats and made few friends with his anti-Semitic remarks. In the end, his opposition to America's anti-Nazi policies led to his resignation in disgrace from his coveted ambassadorship and, for all intents and purposes, ended whatever political career he harbored for himself.

https://warfarehistorynetwork.com/article/joseph-p-kennedy-most-controversial-ambassador-to-great-britain/

In 1938 President Roosevelt appointed John Kennedy to be the ambassador to Britain. In his first speech in England, he declared that it was best for America if it remained neutral in Britain's aim to wage war with Nazi Germany. This was controversial and lost favor with the British people.

War clouds were building over Europe. In September 1938, after the Anschluss with Austria, Adolf Hitler annexed the German-speaking portions of Czechoslovakia, and then, a year later, Hitler's blitzkrieg overran Poland, setting off a major crisis in both London and Paris as to how to respond to Germany's aggression. A year earlier, Britain had given Poland its assurances that if it were attacked by Germany, Britain would come to her aid. In the days and months after the German invasion, neither France nor Britain took any forceful military action against Germany.

In June, Hitler rode triumphantly into Paris, the conquered City of Light. With the fall of France, Britain stood alone against Nazi Germany's tyranny. The United States did not enter the war for another year and a half.

https://warfarehistorynetwork.com/article/joseph-p-kennedy-most-controversial-ambassador-to-great-britain/

The FBI files of John Kennedy.

Due to his temperament, the FBI opened a file on JFK's father.

An FBI memo dated April 28, 1947, from Director Hoover to his aide, D.M. Ladd, gives more information on the Bureau's relationship with Ambassador Kennedy: "In June 1938, Special Agent (Blank) advised that he had received very cordial treatment from Ambassador Kennedy in London, while (Blank) was there visiting Scotland Yard. Kennedy's Ambassadorship to Britain is widely regarded in the United States as demonstrating that Kennedy was an appeaser and believed that Britain would lose the war.

On October 18, 1943, after Kennedy ended his role as ambassador to Great Britain, Hoover wrote the following memo to the special agent in charge in the FBI's Boston office:

"In the event, you feel that Mr. Kennedy is in a position to offer active assistance to the Bureau such as is expected of Special Service Contacts, there is no objection to utilizing him in this capacity. If he can be made use of as a Special Service Contact, the Bureau should be advised as to the nature of the information he can provide, or the facilities he can offer for the Bureau's use. Every effort should be made to provide him with investigative assignments in keeping with his particular ability and the Bureau should be advised of the nature of these assignments, together with the results obtained."

Despite the work that Ambassador Kennedy did for the Bureau (the records do not reflect exactly what he did), Director Hoover "recommended that the meritorious service award not be awarded to Mr. Joseph P. Kennedy for the reason that he has not affirmatively actually done anything of special value to the Bureau despite his willingness to perform such services."

John Kennedy was known for his blatant anti-Semitic remarks.

Something that always raised controversy given his high position as the ambassador to Britain. While in Britain as Ambassador John

Kennedy felt that he was left out of policy formulations and he blamed the State Department for this. He requested to cease being an ambassador to Britain. This might be because President Franklin D Roosevelt might have restricted his involvement because of his anti-Semitic remarks. There was a rift between the President and John Kennedy. He nevertheless endorsed the president but insisted that he felt that the US should mind its economic prosperity and stay away from the European war against the Nazis.

The US sends 50 obsolete destroyers to aid Britain's war in exchange for a military base in the Caribbean.

It can be said that John Kennedy's words against the war were to preserve the lives of his sons. As he knew that if America was involved, then his sons might be sent to fight which they did later with the result of what he feared. The deaths of his children.

Joe Jr was killed in Europe testing a drone craft in August 1944

Lord Granville Leverson Gower.

Granville served as British ambassador to Russia (10 August 1804 – 28 November 1805 and 1806–1807).

William Smith the abolitionist

William Smith (22 September 1756 – 31 May 1835) was a leading independent British politician, sitting as a Member of Parliament (MP) for more than one constituency. He was an English Dissenter and was instrumental in bringing political rights to that religious minority. He was a friend and close associate of William Wilberforce and a member of the Clapham Sect of social reformers and was at the forefront of many of their campaigns for social justice, prison reform, and philanthropic endeavor, most notably the abolition of slavery. He was the grandfather of pioneer nurse and statistician Florence Nightingale and educationalist Barbara Bodichon, a founder of Girton College, Cambridge.

Abolitionism[edit]

In June 1787, Smith was one of the first to campaign for the abolition of the slave trade, becoming a vocal advocate for the cause. In 1790 he supported William Wilberforce in the slave trade debate in April. While he had been out of parliament, he had given his support to Abolitionism by writing a pamphlet entitled A Letter to William Wilberforce (1807), in which he cogently and convincingly summarized the abolitionists' arguments for abolition. Once the trade had been halted, he turned his attention to freeing those who were already slaves. In 1823 Zachary Macaulay helped found the London Society for the Abolition of Slavery in our Colonies, thereby launching the next phase of the campaign to eradicate slavery.

Wikipedia.

Now ladies and gentlemen I have given you the script which our assassin is to use to carry out the same act of assassinating a prime minister or president.

The other assumption is that the assassin does not know that he will kill in the end. Someone who knows this event and has this script will influence character and events so that the assassin will have to do exactly as John Bellingham to arrive at the murder of the prime minister and or president.

8

In comes the Beast.

We can tell that this person or cult, government, or institution must have powers to control and influence events for our assassin to end up killing the prime minister or the president.

But how can someone influence events to such an extent surely lightning can't strike twice at the same place? But this is what the Beast is trying to do. So how can the Beast be able to do all this to control not just one person but several people?

Characteristics of the Beast.

Must be someone, cult, government, or institution in a position of trust. One trusted by many to be believed and influenced most.

One that has the power not just to control but to offer protection as well to the people who did what it wants and one that people can trust enough to keep its secrets. After all, it is the one to kill people or ask others to kill on its behalf and protect these people.

Someone cult or institution that has a global presence to be able to influence events in other countries as well.

Is very advanced that it can somehow control people and be easily obeyed. It must also have advanced technology to control the people directly and forcefully.

It must have strict and very robust rules usually relying on some pledges and oaths of obedience that even if people know that what was asked of them to do was wrong, they will still conceal the identity of this Beast.

In most cases, the subjects or victims must be linked to it.

Using this guideline, we can identify two prominent likely beasts.

Monarchy's

Government institutions that are coordinated like the Hospital, linked to the police, the FBI, and the CIA all work together as the Beast.

Monarchy's

These fit the description for several reasons.

The British monarchy for example through the commonwealth influences several countries in the world.

They have a system of pledges of obedience or oaths of allegiance where secrets are to be kept.

They chip all infants at birth.

i] A GPS tracker.

ii] A black-box chip that enables the recording and playback of conversations and recordings.

iii] A digital chip that enables them to use digital hypnosis where the recordings of a person's voice are replayed back deep in the ear when one is asleep so that the person thinks that he was dreaming. Small inner voices with low decibels are played when a person is deeply asleep. Since it's the person's voice the brain converts these voices' acoustic sounds into visuals so that the person dreams what is being played back. When he wakes up will believe that he was dreaming.

This acts as a communication way but without the person knowing. This is because the dream will come true as the Beast the next day while the dream is still fresh will recreate the dream. Over time the person might start to believe in dreams because what he dreams somehow will come true. [Picture scenes from Final Destination.]

The person will be sure that he saw that dream that went on to happen so from that time will start to believe in dreams so sure that it was a dream.

vi] A rotary function propeller so small that it can be inserted in the lumbar bone to be used to rotate the iris of the eye at ninety degrees so that the iris is hidden in the eye. But we only see because of the iris now imagine when the iris is hidden in the eye socket. How can you see? Picture a driver carrying a monarch having a fatal accident and everything attributed to drinking and driving. What if the driver was digitally hooded; meaning the iris of the eyes were hidden in the eye socket remotely through a joystick or handheld monitor doing 90 miles per hour?

All this is to achieve the events in the script.

Hospitals in England chip all newborn babies at birth. I know I can prove it. It is a fact that all foreign kids in Britain are chipped too, mostly without the consent of the parents secretly to spy on all to protect the monarchy.

All your secrets and conversations are known. They simply listen to all your conversations through your kid's chips if you might suspect this. So, they use the kids where if the kids complain of vibrations, etc in the end they simply say your son is hallucinating. That starts the grooming etc and torture.

vii] They also fire in the left buttock of your kid a needle diode that emits radiation and electricity which they use to torture and command obedience.

But one can argue that in the 1960s the technology was not that advanced, but we have proof that this was so.

Ever heard of the monarchies being part of the reptile? The Reptilian conspiracies.

They are among us. Blood-drinking, flesh-eating, shape-shifting extraterrestrial reptilian humanoids with only one objective in their cold-blooded little heads: to enslave the human race. They are our leaders, our corporate executives, our beloved Oscar-winning actors, and Grammy-winning singers, and they're responsible for the Holocaust, the Oklahoma City bombings, and the 9/11 attacks ... at least according to former BBC sports reporter David Icke, who became the poster human for the theory in 1998 after publishing his first book, The Biggest Secret, which contained interviews with two Brits who claimed members of the royal family are nothing more than reptiles with crowns. (Picture Dracula meets Swamp Thing).

https://content.time.com/time/specials/packages/article/0,28804,18 60871_1860876_1861029,00.html

I will tell you why they are regarded as reptile conspiracy theories. This is because they use sophisticated gadgets to pull the iris of the eye to the sides so that the iris goes to the sides instead of the center all the time unless a person is looking at an angle.

All this is due to this rotary miniature propeller that moves the iris to the sides.

The biggest question to ask is the fact that was the president of the United States JFK tampered with by the British.

It is a fact that he grew up in England when his father was the ambassador to Britain. So, he might have been chipped by the British without consent or his parents knowing. Especially the fact that his father was against aiding the British against the Nazi Germany. He believed that "Democracy was finished in Britain". He believed that Britain was going to rescue the Poles not for democracy but for self-gain and preservation. I pointed out in my other books that King Edward I of England 1274 introduced the

Edict of Eviction. That saw the persecution of Jews. Adolf Hitler, we believe, simply played the King Edward I script of persecuting the Jews. So, the British went to rescue the Poles to cover their tracks.

It can be argued that JFK's father was against the war simply to protect his kids and his boys who were in the army. Kids later went on to die because of the war. He might not have been against the war but having so many kids in the army surely would make any father stand against the war. To protect his kids.

Another proof is JFK's speech about the enemy within.

What can you do when you discover that the people you trusted your British doctor with the help of the hospital inserted the kit above as a kid? Imagine JFK years after their return to the UK discovering that he was implanted with a chip that is used to listen to all his conversations. A chip that is used to snoop through a video sender all his phone screens and laptop and computer screens.

Imagine the British knowing exactly how he made love to Marylin Monroe. How did he fart and how many times? Above all trapped without knowing what to do. If he says the British hacked him when he was young people will say he is mad and hallucinating.

All the FBI and CIA are just the puppets of the British queen hacked as well. All can't fight the British. Who can he tell that the British are accusing him of treason for standing for justice?

But how can he tell the world that all his pains and troubles are because of the chip inserted by the British secretly?

If he cries foul play, even the FBI will accuse him of hallucinating. Not because that is what they believe, no. Just because they are all puppets of the British. Hallucinating even more than him.

This was echoed by his brother Robert F Kennedy who ended up being gunned down as well.

The Enemy Within The McClellan Committee's Crusade Against Jimmy Hoffa and Corrupt Labor Unions is a book by American politician Robert F. Kennedy [1] (assisted by John Seigenthaler)[2] first published in 1960 and republished in 1994. [3] Edwin Guthman, chairman of the Robert F. Kennedy Memorial, provided the introduction to the 1994 edition. [3] As Robert Kennedy was intimately involved, the book is somewhat autobiographical.

The hospitals with the help of the FBI and CIA can be the Beast as well.

We know the CIA uses young prostitutes to get the men they are after hacked as well where the hospitals kill the parents of the child to be groomed by the teaching hospitals. Then recreate a past event to set up the person who might be a threat to the monarchy. Above all, they have all the evil gadgets the monarchies have.

We know for a fact the FBI had a file on JFK's father.

The questions to ask here are these.

Was JFK a pain to the FBI?

Was JFK an embarrassment to the establishment?

If yes, then the FBI might have considered his position as an embarrassment enough to trigger Lee Harvey Oswald to act as John Bellingham to kill him.

You just understand that at this point it can't be Lee Harvey Oswald doing everything to end up killing President JFK.

Even if he is the one who killed the president, there was someone who was controlling the events step by step. Oswald was like a puppet on strings being jerked on all sides to make the right moves.

So outright even if Lee Harvey Oswald pulled the trigger it was not him the killer of the president. Someone else was behind the scenes running the script of John Bellingham to make sure that in the end, Oswald pulled the trigger just like John Bellingham.

But was Lee Harvey Oswald in the same position as John Bellingham?

9

The Comparison. Lee Harvey Oswald versus John Bellingham.

To fit the assassin's personality Lee Harvey Oswald must match the personality and circumstances of John Bellingham.

John Bellingham had his problems in Russia where he was imprisoned for six years.

Lee Harvey Oswald was detained here in the US before leaving for Russia. It can be said that Lee Harvey Oswald did not face the harsh conditions of prison as experienced by John Bellingham.

For argument's sake, we can assume that the mistreatment Lee Harvey Oswald suffered was here in the United States in the army when he was imprisoned. Factors that made him leave for Russia.

Bellingham worked as a clerk in a counting house in the late 1790s, and in about 1800 he went to Arkhangelsk, Russia, as an agent for importers and exporters. He returned to England in 1802 and was a merchant broker in Liverpool. He married Mary Neville in 1803. In the summer of 1804, Bellingham again went to Arkhangelsk to work as an export representative.

Lee Harvey Oswald when he was 17, joined the Marines. Oswald was court-martialed twice while in the Marines and jailed. He was honorably released from active duty in the Marine Corps into the Marine Corps Reserve, then flew to Europe and defected to the Soviet Union in October 1959. He lived in Minsk, Byelorussia, married a Russian woman named Marina and had a daughter. In June 1962, he returned to the United States with his wife, and eventually settled in Dallas, where their second daughter was born.

John Bellingham was accused of frustrating an insurance payout and as such was made liable for debt worth $2000 which he denied. That led to his imprisonment. With the issue still unresolved, Bellingham obtained passes for him and his family to travel to the Russian capital, St Petersburg. In February 1805, as they prepared to set out, Bellingham's pass was revoked; Mary and the child were permitted to proceed, but he was arrested and imprisoned in Archangel. When he sought help from Lord Granville Leveson-Gower, the British ambassador in St Petersburg, the matter was dealt with by the British consul, Sir Stephen Sharp, who informed Bellingham that as the dispute involved a civil debt, he could not interfere.

There is no proof that Oswald suffered ill-treatment in Russia; he was blessed with a wife and baby. We can only assume that if he suffered any ill-treatment, it was either before he left for Russia or when he came back.

Bellingham remained in custody in Archangel until November 1805, when a new city governor ordered his release and allowed him to join Mary in St Petersburg. Here, instead of arranging his family's swift return to England, Bellingham laid charges against the Archangel authorities for false imprisonment and demanded compensation.

It can be said that John Bellingham as a businessman strongly believed in compensation when he ever felt wrong. But this is the reason why he ended up in problems.

In doing so he outraged the Russian authorities, who in June 1806 ordered his imprisonment. [35] According to his later account, Bellingham was "often marched publicly through the city with gangs of felons and criminals of the worst description [to the] heart-rending humiliation of himself".

Mary had meanwhile returned to England with her son (she was pregnant with her second child), eventually settling in Liverpool where she set up a millinery business with a friend, Mary Stevens.

Like all Marines, Oswald was trained and tested in the shooting. In December 1956, he scored 212, which was slightly above the requirements for the designation of sharpshooter. [20] In May 1959 he scored 191, which reduced his rating to the marksman.

Oswald was court-martialed after he accidentally shot himself in the elbow with an unauthorized .22 caliber handgun. He was court-martialed a second time for fighting with a sergeant who he thought was responsible for his punishment in the shooting matter. He was demoted from private first class to private and briefly imprisoned. Oswald was later punished for a third incident: while he was on night-time sentry duty in the Philippines, he inexplicably fired his rifle into the jungle.

After marrying Marina Prusakova, the US Embassy gave a loan to Oswald of $435.71. Opposite to the denial of help John Bellingham experienced.

The Oswalds soon settled in the Dallas/Fort Worth area, where Lee's mother and brother lived.

Marina, meanwhile, befriended Ruth Paine,[83] a Quaker trying to learn Russian, and her husband Michael Paine, who worked for Bell Helicopter. [84].

On his return to England, Bellingham spent six months in London, seeking compensation for the imprisonment and financial losses he had suffered in Russia. He considered the British authorities to be responsible for their neglect of his repeated requests for help. Successively he petitioned the Foreign Office, the Treasury, the Privy Council, and Perceval himself; [41] in each case his claims were politely rejected. Defeated and exhausted, in May 1811 Bellingham accepted his wife's ultimatum to abandon his campaign or otherwise lose her and his family. He joined her in

Liverpool to begin life afresh. [42]

Detailed Background Notes of Events [extracts from Wikipedia.]

In December 1811 Bellingham returned to London, ostensibly to conduct business there, but in reality, to resume his campaign for redress. [43] He petitioned the Prince Regent [44] before resuming his efforts with the Privy Council, the Home Office, and the Treasury, only to receive the same polite refusals as before. [45] He then sent a copy of his petition to every member of Parliament, again to no avail.[46] On 23 March 1812, Bellingham wrote to the magistrates at Bow Street Magistrates' Court, arguing that the government had "completely endeavored to close the door of justice",[47] and asking the court to intervene.

After consulting his MP, Isaac Gascoyne, Bellingham made a final attempt to present his case to the government. On 18 April, he met with a Treasury official, Mr. Hill, to whom he said that if he could get no satisfaction, he would take justice into his own hands. Hill, not perceiving these words as a threat, told him he should take whatever action he deemed proper. [48] On 20 April, Bellingham purchased two .50 caliber (12.7 mm) pistols from a gunsmith of 58 Skinner Street. He also had a tailor sew an inside pocket to his coat. [49]

In March 1963, Oswald used the alias "A. Hidell" to make a mail-order purchase of a second-hand 6.5 mm caliber Carcano rifle for $29.95. [87] He also purchased a .38 Smith & Wesson Model 10 revolver by the same method. [88] The Warren Commission concluded that Oswald attempted to kill retired U.S. Major General Edwin Walker on April 10, 1963 and that Oswald fired the Carcano rifle at Walker through a window from less than 100 feet (30 m) away as Walker sat at a desk in his Dallas home. The bullet struck the window frame and Walker's only injuries were bullet fragments to the forearm.

Frustration and lack of redress made John Bellingham buy two guns. Whereas Lee Harvey Oswald's discrimination he suffered as a communist sympathizer made him purchase two revolvers using the name A Hidell.

General Walker was an outspoken anti-communist, segregationist, and member of the John Birch Society.

Marina Oswald testified that her husband told her that he traveled by bus to General Walker's house and shot at Walker with his rifle. [94][95] She said that Oswald considered Walker to be the leader of a "fascist organization".

Oswald returned to New Orleans on April 24, 1963. [109] Marina's friend Ruth Paine drove her by car from Dallas to join Oswald in New Orleans the following month.

New Orleans District Attorney Jim Garrison claimed that Oswald spent that time across the street at 544 Camp Street. These were the law offices of Guy Banister, a former FBI agent, an avid segregationist, and a local politician. Garrison added that Guy Banister during the summer of 1963 in New Orleans, was most interested in infiltrating the Fair Play for Cuba Committee, and used Oswald as his spy.

On May 26, Oswald wrote to the New York City headquarters of the pro-Fidel Castro Fair Play for Cuba Committee, proposing to rent "a small office at my own expense to form an FPCC branch here in New Orleans".[115] Three days later, the FPCC responded to Oswald's letter advising against opening a New Orleans office "at least not ... at the very beginning".[116] In a follow-up letter, Oswald replied, "Against your advice, I have decided to take an office from the very beginning."

On May 29, Oswald ordered the following items from a local printer: 500 application forms, 300 membership cards, and 1,000 leaflets with the heading, "Hands Off Cuba".[118] According to Marina, Lee told her to sign the name "A.J. Hidell" as chapter president on his membership card.

Oswald fought with Bringer, the anti-Castro campaigner. This led to his arrest and before leaving the police he asked to speak to an FBI agent.

Oswald requested to speak with an FBI agent. [123] Oswald told the agent that he was a member of the New Orleans branch of the Fair Play for Cuba Committee which he claimed had 35 members and was led by A. J. Hidell. [123] In fact, Oswald was the branch's only member and it had never been chartered by the national organization. [124]

A week later, on August 16, Oswald again passed out Fair Play for Cuba leaflets with two hired helpers, this time in front of the International Trade Mart. The incident was filmed by WDSU, a local TV station.

Marina's friend Ruth Paine transported Marina and her child by car from New Orleans to the Paine home in Irving, Texas, near Dallas, on September 23, 1963.

Oswald is believed to have traveled to Mexico to get visas for Russia instead of going to Dallas where Marine was.

He was denied a Cuban visa when he returned to Dallas. But his visa was approved on October 18 and by this time he was back in the US.

By 2 October 1963 Oswald had returned to the US. Ruth Paine, his wife's friend, had found a job for Oswald at the Texas School Depository where her neighbor's brother, Wesley Frazier.

Here we see the similarity to John Bellingham. The need for constant presence to raise no suspicion on the day of the attack.

People had seen John Bellingham petitioning ministers and journalists. Now we see Oswald with a constant presence at the Texas School Book Depository.

Wikipedia.

Oswald stayed at Dallas roaming house weekdays and weekends and went to Ruth Paine's house where his wife was.

On October 20 (a month before the assassination), Oswald's second daughter, Audrey, was born. I would like to believe that this is the critical point that made Oswald a threat to the president FBI, etc. This is because the birth of a child triggers masculine instincts of protecting its young ones at any cost.

I can't see why he would match the suffering that John Bellingham suffered during his time in a Russian prison.

Especially the fact. The Dallas branch of the FBI became interested in Oswald after its agent learned that the CIA had determined that Oswald had been in contact with the Soviet embassy in Mexico, making Oswald a possible espionage case.

The critical point is when the FBI agents twice visited the Paine home in early November when Oswald was not present and spoke to Mrs. Paine.

This is the trigger of the problems to follow. Especially considering the hatred towards communists and the discrimination his wife had suffered in the local neighborhood of Dallas. Surely any male would kill to protect the mother and the young babies is it from the FBI or any anti-segregationist?

Oswald visited the Dallas FBI office about two to three weeks before the assassination, asking to see Special Agent James P. Hosty.

Here we have similarities with John Bellingham. The issues have become so critical that he has to make his presence be felt as he seeks redress.

Hosty was not there so Oswald left a note that read.

"Let this be a warning. I will blow up the FBI and the Dallas Police Department if you don't stop bothering my wife" [signed] "Lee Harvey Oswald." The note allegedly contained a threat, but accounts vary as to whether Oswald threatened to "blow up the FBI" or merely "report this to higher authorities". According to Hosty, the note said, "If you have anything you want to learn about me, come talk to me directly. If you don't cease bothering my wife, I will take the appropriate action and report this to the proper authorities." Agent Hosty said that he destroyed Oswald's note on orders from his superior, Gordon Shanklin after Oswald was named the suspect in the Kennedy assassination. [148][149]

So far this point matches that of John Bellingham in that at this point after frustrations the men Oswald and Bellingham are fed up and now are threatening to take the law into their own hands as the only option to redress left. But the situation makes the threats look not so serious. But these two men are fed up, and this acts as the trigger of what followers. This lack of justice is the turning point. These two men now from this point realize that there is never going to be any redress. The only redress is to take the law into its own hands and deliver justice.

Another point is the fact that no one takes them seriously. John Bellingham, they believe that surely, he can't harm a fly because if he did, he would have done it by now. His calmness and composure and the fact that he was always there erase any suspicion.

I believe John Bellingham might have genuine reasons to end

someone's life. Imprisoned for six years when you could have easily been bailed out is hard to comprehend especially after John argued that he never broke any laws or killed anyone, yet he spent six years in a rat-infested jail. So surely John had every reason to blast the British Ambassador to Russia or even the prime minister.

But Oswald's reasons are not that convincing but looking at the discrimination his wife suffered and his inability to do anything about this to stop this abuse might have enraged him. Dallas as we know was anti-communist and against non-segregation.

Both men are challenged to do whatever they can but to the authorities that would not change anything their judgment was final. Frustrated, given no other option these men both told the authorities as it is.

Fuck up with this powerful movement and pay the consequences but all complacent and not understanding what was going on behind the scene underestimated the two men. To them, both these men gave them jobs and something to look forward to. Their salaries, etc. The more they complained the more jobs and salaries they had. But these men were fed up.

In the days before Kennedy's arrival, several local newspapers published the route of Kennedy's motorcade, which passed the Texas School Book Depository. [150] On Thursday, November 21, 1963, Oswald asked Frazier for an unusual mid-week lift back to Irving, saying he had to pick up some curtain rods. The next morning (the day of the assassination), he returned to Dallas with Frazier. He left $170 and his wedding ring,[151] but took a large paper bag with him. Frazier reported that Oswald told him the bag contained curtain rods. [152][153] The Warren Commission concluded that the package of "curtain rods" contained the rifle that Oswald was going to use for the assassination.

*After taking a friend's family to a painting exhibition on 11 May
1812, Bellingham remarked that he had some business to attend to.
He made his way to Parliament, where he waited in the lobby.
When Prime Minister Spencer Perceval appeared, Bellingham
stepped forward and shot him in the heart. He then calmly sat on a
bench.*

Wikipedia.

In an FBI report taken the day after the assassination, Givens said
that the encounter took place at 11:30 a.m. and that he saw Oswald
reading a newspaper in the first-floor domino room at 11:50 a.m.,
20 minutes later.

*As Kennedy's motorcade passed through Dealey Plaza at
approximately 12:30 p.m. on November 22, Oswald fired three
rifle shots from the southeast-corner window on the sixth floor of
the Texas School Book Depository,[164] killing the President and
seriously wounding Texas Governor John Connally. One shot
missed the presidential limousine entirely, another struck both
Kennedy and Connally, and a third bullet struck Kennedy in the
head,[165] killing him. Bystander James Tague received a minor
facial injury from a small piece of curbstone that had fragmented
after it was struck by one of the bullets.*

*The paper bag Frazier had described was found by police near the
open sixth-floor window from which Oswald was determined to
have fired; [153] it was 38 inches (97 cm) long and had marks on
its inside consistent with having been used to carry a rifle. [153] A
Mannlicher-Carcano rifle and three shell casings were found near
the window as well.*

*About 90 seconds after the shots sounded, he was encountered in
the second-floor lunchroom by Dallas police officer Marion L.
Baker, who was with Oswald's supervisor, Roy Truly. Baker let*

Oswald pass after Truly identified him as an employee. Baker later said Oswald did not seem "nervous" or "out of breath".

Here we see critical similarities in that Oswald as a grieved man probably because of the abuse he suffered in the US before he left for Russia was burned on revenge that he would not hesitate to take the president's life. Just like John who felt neglected in Russia's jail felt no remorse in blasting the Prime Minister. Both men feeling vindicated and justified did not panic but calmly without running away stood around or even sat down.

Mrs. Robert Reid, a clerical supervisor at the depository who returned to her office within two minutes of the shooting, said she saw Oswald, "very calm", on the second floor holding a Coca-Cola bottle. [178] As they walked past each other, Mrs. Reid said to Oswald, "The President has been shot" to which he mumbled something in response, but Reid did not understand him. [179] Oswald was believed to have left the depository through the front entrance just before police sealed it off. Truly later pointed out to officers that Oswald was the only employee that he was certain was missing.

Wikipedia.

Recall that John Bellingham sat down on the bench to vindicate that justice had been done by his hand. The shot men deserved it. It was only a result of their arrogance and thinking that they were above the law. But these men were to prove them wrong that no one was above the law. President or prime minister.

What a turn of events that the most powerful men are easily killed by common men without anything but pain in their hearts and the guts to pull the trigger. All this in the name of justice and a clear message to all these bastards out there that making your wishes the law will inevitably bring personal risk to these men.

Tippit pulled alongside Oswald and "apparently exchanged words with [him] through the right front or vent window".[189] "Shortly after 1:15 p.m.", [n 10] Tippit exited his car. Oswald immediately fired his pistol and killed the policeman with four shots. [189][190] Numerous witnesses heard the shots and saw Oswald flee the scene holding a revolver; nine positively identified him as the man who shot Tippit and fled. [191][n 11] Four cartridge cases found at the scene were identified by expert witnesses[192] before the Warren Commission and the House Select Committee as having been fired from the revolver later found in Oswald's possession, excluding all other weapons. The bullets taken from Tippit's body could not be positively identified as having been fired from Oswald's revolver, as the bullets were too extensively damaged to make conclusive assessments. [192][193].

Shoe store manager Johnny Brewer testified that he saw Oswald "ducking into" the entrance alcove of his store. Suspicious of this activity, Brewer watched Oswald continue up the street and slip without paying into the nearby Texas Theater, where the film War Is Hell was playing. [194] He alerted the theater's ticket clerk, who telephoned police [195] at about 1:40 p.m.

As police arrived, the house lights were brought up and Brewer pointed out Oswald sitting near the rear of the theater. Police Officer Nick McDonald testified that he was the first to reach Oswald, and that Oswald seemed ready to surrender saying, "Well, it is all over now."

Before the prisoner was called on regularly to plead, Mr. Alley, his counsel, made an application to have the trial postponed, to procure proof of his client's insanity, which was alleged in two affidavits he held: he said that he had no doubt, if time were allowed, that the prisoner could be proved to be insane. Mr. Alley was here interrupted by the court, who refused to hear him until the prisoner had first pleaded.

The indictment was then read, and the usual question, 'Guilty, or not guilty?' was put to Bellingham, when he addressed the court: 'My lords -- Before I can plead to this indictment, I must state, in justice to myself, that by hurrying on my trial I am placed in a most remarkable situation. It so happens that my prosecutors are the witnesses against me. All the documents on which alone I could rest my defense have been taken from me and are now in possession of the Crown. It is only two days since I was told to prepare for my defense, and when I asked for my papers, I was told they could not be given up. It is, therefore, my lords, rendered utterly impossible for me to go into my justification, and under the circumstances in which I find myself, a trial is useless. The papers are to be given to me after the trial, but how can that avail me for my defense? I am, therefore, not ready for my trial.'

Wikipedia.

https://www.exclassics.com/newgate/ng550.htm

As he was led from the theater, Oswald shouted he was a victim of police brutality.

Soon after his arrest, Oswald encountered reporters in a hallway. Oswald declared, "I didn't shoot anybody" and, "They've taken me in because I lived in the Soviet Union. I'm just a patsy!"

This is very critical to our hypothesis. To match the assassin Oswald to match John Bellingham must have lived in the Soviet Union. Russia. The place where all the ill-treatment must have happened. But in Oswald's case, Russia can be said to have been a blessing. He found a wife, unlike John Bellingham who spent six years in prison. To him, his sin was that he was in the Soviet Union.

The Beast might have told the people that all this is happening because the assassin was in the Soviet Union. So, like John

Bellingham, he was killed as revenge for the neglect. But this is not the case with Oswald. So, he explained that he was just a patsy just because he was in the Soviet Union.

Just like in the trial of Bellingham he was asked if guilty or not by a reporter who asked. "Did you kill the President?" and Oswald who by that time had been advised of the charge of murdering Tippit, but had not yet been arraigned in Kennedy's death – answered, "No, I have not been charged with that. Nobody has said that to me yet. The first thing I heard about it was when the newspaper reporters in the hall asked me that question."[202] As he was led from the room the question was called out, "What did you do in Russia?" and, "How did you hurt your eye?"; Oswald answered, "A policeman hit me."[199] By early the next morning (shortly after 1:30 a.m.) he had been arraigned for the assassination of President Kennedy. [203]

Oswald denied killing Kennedy and Tippit, denied owning a rifle, and said two photographs of him holding a rifle and a pistol were fakes. He denied telling his co-worker he wanted a ride to Irving to get curtain rods for his apartment (he said that the package contained his lunch). He also denied carrying a long, bulky package to work the morning of the assassination. Oswald denied knowing an "A. J. Hidell". Oswald was then shown a forged Selective Service System card bearing his photograph and the alias, "Alek James Hidell" which he had in his possession at the time of his arrest. Oswald refused to answer any questions concerning the card, saying "you have the card yourself and you know as much about it as I do"

Lee Harvey Oswald and Alek James Hidell.

So many theories surrounded the use of two names by Oswald. Some suggested a split personality disorder.

Did Lee Harvey Oswald conceive of himself as a split personality—a better side struggling against an eviller nature?

Was the pseudonym used by the assassin of President Kennedy a reflection of such a recognition of himself—an attempt at an anagram, subconscious or intentional?

In the effort to decipher the puzzles in the strange career of Oswald, there has been speculation about the false name he used, "Alek J. Hidell."

Various suggestions have regarded the pseudonym as possibly influenced by the Jekyll and Hyde characters of Robert Louis Stevenson.

Lee Harvey Oswald could have claimed compensation for the imprisonment he suffered in the USA in the military where he was imprisoned. But the government after tricking him to make fake IDS in the name of Alek James Hidell then use this information to disapprove his story of being in the army or any compensation claims after being imprisoned in the US before going to Russia.

Or he claimed for the problems he suffered in Russia because of the embassy taking his passport, etc. Whatever the reason was he had sought some form of redress just like John Bellingham.

Instead, the government dismissed his claim on grounds that he didn't qualify; they used forgery of documents to dismiss his rights to compensation, insurance, or any help.

Just like John Bellingham, he did not run as expected, instead he acted the way he did so that the police would come to the theater to arrest him. After going back to his place to collect the other ID as he was found with both IDS. That could also explain why he replied the way he did when he was asked about the name Alek James Hidell.

Selective Selection System Insurance: compensation and refusal to pay out because he forged IDS. Caught with two ids with his photo and two different names the government refused to pay.

Trigger for him to blast all.

But I think the selective Selection System has something to do with insurance.

Registering this Selective Service System meant some guarantees of work; help funding etc within the federal government.

I know that Marina probably agreed to go with Ruth Paine because she knows Oswald was broke. He had stayed in Orleans to collect a government subsidy of $33. Instead of going to Dallas with his wife. He instead used the money to go to Mexico to try to get visas back to the Soviet Union. Work hard has been hard to secure. He had thought that he would have been insured or guaranteed work with this Selective Service System, but the FBI might have tricked him, especially this Guy Banister.

New Orleans District Attorney Jim Garrison claimed that Oswald spent that time across the street at 544 Camp Street. These were the law offices of Guy Banister, a former FBI agent, an avid segregationist, and a local politician. Garrison added that Guy Banister during the summer of 1963 in New Orleans, was most interested in infiltrating the Fair Play for Cuba Committee, and used Oswald as his spy.

We know that work was tough after returning to the US. The FBI especially this Guy Banister to make him more destitute pretended to offer him a job to work as a spy. That means trying to infiltrate the Fair Play for Cuba Committee. This means using an alias. Another name in the process fortifies any benefits of the Selective Service System as now he will be accused of fraudulent forgery etc as now he has two cards with his photos but different names. A very good reason why the Federal government would refuse to pay out whatever that card entitles one.

A man with a young family who had everything to be tricked like this can become very angry. The FBI had taken advantage of him at his lowest point to take a little help he had been entitled to by this Selective Service System.

That would make him teach someone a lesson.

The FBI would have done this so that they open a file on him for forgery so that they follow him. Probably the reason why they visited his wife or wife's friend to confirm that he had forged a card and that was the reason why the government refused any payouts. Instead of going to his wife in Dallas after collecting a $33 unemployment check, he decided to go to get a visa.

As the FBI speculated that he escaped after blasting the president.

NB

The Warren Commission examined the capabilities of the Carcano rifle and ammunition, as well as Oswald's military training and post-military experience, and determined that Oswald could fire three shots within a period of 4.8 to 5.6 seconds. [227] According to their report, an army specialist using Oswald's rifle was able to duplicate the feat and even improved on the time. The report also states that the Army Infantry Weapons Evaluation Branch test-fired Oswald's rifle 47 times and found that it was "quite accurate", comparing it to the accuracy of an M14 rifle. Also contained in the Commission report is testimony by Marine Corps Major Eugene Anderson confirming that Oswald's military records show that he qualified as a "sharpshooter" in 1956.

Several FBI employees had made statements indicating that Oswald was indeed a paid informant, but the Commission was

nonetheless unable to verify the veracity of those claims.
[242][243] FBI agent James Hosty reported that his office's
interactions with Oswald were limited to dealing with his
complaints about being harassed by the Bureau for being a
communist sympathizer. In the weeks before the assassination,
Oswald made a personal visit to the FBI's Dallas branch office
with a hand-delivered letter that purportedly contained a threat of
some sort but, controversially, Hosty destroyed the letter by order
of J. Gordon Shanklin, his supervisor. [244][245][246]

Wikipedia.

Bear this in mind about the Beast I talked about. The FBI to
control him and force him to kill JFK tricked him to act as an
infiltrating spy. Meaning he had to forge documents as Marina
later testified.

On May 29, Oswald ordered the following items from a local
printer: 500 application forms, 300 membership cards, and 1,000
leaflets with the heading, "Hands Off Cuba".[118] According to
Marina, Lee told her to sign the name "A.J. Hidell" as chapter
president on his membership card.

Oswald even received a repatriation loan from the State
Department [

Whatever followed had nothing to do with him being suspected of
being a spy of the Soviet Union but proof that he had forged the
Selective Service System cards fortified any insurance benefits
hence the government refused to pay out. A hungry man with a
family is an angry man especially tricked like this. The FBI might
have done this deliberately to make him mad.

All the visits by the FBI were to escalate the situation. He might
have lied to his wife promising her an insurance pay-out or help of
some kind, but the FBI might have spilled the beans. Now exposed

that he lied to his wife ashamed he leaves his wedding ring. Apologizing for lying to her and getting a rifle to get even.

The government had refused to pay but he would make them pay one way or the other.

On August 9, Oswald turned up in downtown New Orleans handing out pro-Castro leaflets. Bringuier confronted Oswald, claiming he was tipped off about Oswald's leafleting by a friend. A scuffle ensued and Oswald, Bringuier, and two of Bringuier's friends were arrested for disturbing the peace. [121][122] Before leaving the police station, Oswald requested to speak with an FBI agent. [123] Oswald told the agent that he was a member of the New Orleans branch of the Fair Play for Cuba Committee which he claimed had 35 members and was led by A. J. Hidell. [123] In fact, Oswald was the branch's only member and it had never been chartered by the national organization. [124]

A week later, on August 16, Oswald again passed out Fair Play for Cuba leaflets with two hired helpers, this time in front of the International Trade Mart. The incident was filmed by WDSU, a local TV station. [125] The next day, Oswald was interviewed by WDSU radio commentator William Stuckey, who probed Oswald's background. [126][127] A few days later, Oswald accepted Stuckey's invitation to take part in a radio debate with Carlos Bringuier and Bringuier's associate Edward Scannell Butler, head of the right-wing Information Council of the Americas (INCA). [1

All this had nothing to do with spying but with benefit or insurance fraud. Or to do with debt he owed someone that he could not pay.

Did Oswald owe someone money at that time? Rent to the Paine family, Ruth and Michael? Hoping to get money from the government but his forgery being pointed as the reason for the refusal?

Was John Bellingham Working Alone?

The official conclusion from Bellingham's trial was that Bellingham acted on his own, and the assassination of Spencer Perceval was the culmination of years of refusals for aid from the government. Throughout his trial, Bellingham never wavered in his statement that he was not a part of a larger plot. And yet, starving workers, and others affected by Perceval's policies, rejoiced at the news of Perceval's death. They blessed and thanked Bellingham for ridding the country of Perceval and regretted that he had not taken out other disliked members of Parliament when he had the chance. Spencer Perceval's support of the 1807 Orders in Council, repeal of the Statute of Artificers, a crackdown on Luddite activities, and general inhibition of world trade had made him no shortage of enemies, at home and abroad.

Bellingham's trial was cut and dry. He was seen shooting Perceval by several witnesses and there was no question of who committed the crime. However, there is a small sticking point. How did John Bellingham afford the guns? As a supposedly impoverished man, it is curious that Bellingham was able to pay his bills given how desperate he was to obtain financial restitution from the government.

Some people believe that John Bellingham had sponsors like Thomas Wilson, and American merchant, Elisha Peck. Who were the merchants from Liverpool? These merchants had suffered greatly from Spencer Perceval's policies. This is evidenced by the rejoicing after they learned of his death.

It is believed that even though John Bellingham acted alone, there is still a possibility that the strict policies of Spencer Perceval were at some stage going to trigger some form of uprising or assassination and that John acted first but an event that would nevertheless happen anywhere.

https://www.catostreetconspiracy.org.uk/the-plot/john-bellingham-lone-assassin-or-unwitting-patsy-in-a-larger-conspiracy

John Bellingham: Lone Assassin or Unwitting Patsy in a Larger Conspiracy | Researching the Conspiracy - The Cato Street Conspiracy

Spencer Perceval is best known as the only Prime Minister to be assassinated in British history. But what about his killer? Was John Bellingham simply a desperate last act from a desperate man, or was there a larger plot afoot?

www.catostreetconspiracy.org.uk

The trail of John Bellinghamfrom Wikipedia.

Bellingham's trial began at the Old Bailey on Friday 15 May 1812, under the presiding judge Sir James Mansfield, Chief Justice of the Court of Common Pleas. [83] The prosecuting team was led by the Attorney General, Gibbs, whose assistants included William Garrow, himself a future Attorney General. [84][85] Brougham having declined, Bellingham was represented by Alley, assisted by Henry Revell Reynolds. [83] The law at that time limited the role of defense counsel in capital cases; they could advise on points of law and could examine and cross-examine witnesses, but otherwise, Bellingham would have to present his defense.

Sir James Mansfield, [played by Jack Ruby] SL KC (originally Manfield; 1734 – 23 November 1821) was a British lawyer, judge, and politician. He was twice Solicitor General and served as Chief Justice of the Common Pleas from 1799 to 1814. Mansfield resigned on 21 February 1814, due to ill health and died at his house in London on 23 May 1821.

[Google and compare the drawing of the judge who tried John Bellingham and the picture of Jack Ruby. A spitting image. Coincide? Do you know the works of the beast? Before you proceed with this download both and paste both onto one page using paint and see the resemblance. I told you the Beast uses drawings and pictures to find look alikes. Unbelievable.]

Jack Leon Ruby (born Jacob Leon Rubenstein; April 25, 1911 – January 3, 1967) was an American nightclub owner and alleged associate of the Chicago Outfit who murdered Lee Harvey Oswald on November 24, 1963, two days after Oswald was accused of the assassination of President John F. Kennedy. A Dallas jury found Ruby guilty of murdering Oswald and sentenced him to death. Ruby's conviction was later repealed, and he was to be granted a new trial; however, he became ill in prison and died of a pulmonary embolism from lung cancer on January 3, 1967.

In September 1964, the Warren Commission concluded that Ruby acted alone in killing Oswald, shooting him on impulse, and out of grief over Kennedy's assassination. These findings were challenged by various critics who suggest that Ruby was involved with major figures in organized crime and that he was acting as part of an overall plot surrounding the assassination of Kennedy.

After Bellingham had entered a not-guilty plea, Alley asked for a postponement to allow him time to locate witnesses who could attest to the prisoner's insanity. This was opposed by Gibbs as a mere ploy to delay justice; Mansfield concurred, and the trial proceeded.

Having described the shooting, Gibbs dismissed the possibility of insanity, maintaining that Bellingham was, at the time of the deed, fully in control of his actions.

Wikipedia.

The court also heard from a tailor who, shortly before the attack had, on Bellingham's instructions, modified the latter's coat by adding a special inside pocket, in which Bellingham had concealed his pistols.

Bear in mind how Jack Ruby shot Lee Harvey Oswald.

When Bellingham rose, he thanked the attorney general for rejecting the "insanity" strategy: "I think it is far more fortunate that such a plea ... should have been unfounded than it should have existed in fact"

It can be inferred that the mark on Oswald's forehead could have been deliberately caused by the policeman to suggest to reporters that he was insane, the fact he refused as he pointed out that the policeman had punched him.

He began his defense by asserting that "all the miseries which human nature can endure" had fallen on him.

In his view the principal blame lay not with "that truly amiable and highly lamented individual, Mr. Perceval", but with Leveson-Gower, the ambassador in St Petersburg who he felt had originally denied him justice, and who he said deserved the shot rather than the eventual victim. [95]

Mansfield then began his summing up, during which he clarified the law:

"The single question is whether at the time this act was committed, he possessed a sufficient degree of understanding to distinguish good from evil, right from wrong."[98]

The judge advised the jury before they retired that the evidence showed Bellingham to be "in every respect a full and competent judge of all his actions".[99]

This is the same approach adopted by Jack Ruby. He did not need any evidence. He had judged Lee Harvey Oswald that any man can tell that it is wrong to kill a prime minister or president. As such he had tried Oswald and judged him that he waited after three days to blast him.

Judge Mansfield, damned the crime "as odious and abominable in the eyes of God as it is hateful and abhorrent to the feelings of man".[100] He reminded the prisoner of the short time, "a very short time",[102] that remained for him to seek for mercy in another world, and then pronounced the sentence of death itself:

"You shall be hanged by the neck until you are dead, your body to be dissected and anatomized."[103]

The entire trial lasted less than eight hours.

For the judgment of "your body to be dissected and anatomized" Jack Ruby fired a shot at close range to destroy all vital organs. This meant that Oswald had all his body parts damaged and dissected to verify the damage by the bullet.

 Large crowds gathered outside Newgate Prison on 18 May; a force of troops stood by since warnings had been received of a "Rescue Bellingham" movement. [108] The crowd was calm and restrained, as was Bellingham when he appeared at the scaffold shortly before 8 o'clock. Hodgson records that Bellingham mounted the steps "with the utmost celerity ... his tread was bold and firm ... no indication of trembling, faltering, or irresolution appeared".[109] Bellingham was then blindfolded, the rope fastened, and a final prayer was said by the chaplain. As the clock struck eight the trap door was released, and Bellingham dropped to his death.

Following the court's sentence, the body was cut down and sent to St Bartholomew's Hospital for dissection. [111] In what the press described as "morbid sensationalism", Bellingham's clothes were sold for high prices to members of the public.

After Spencer Perceval's death.

On 8 June, the Regent appointed Lord Liverpool to head a new Tory administration. [114] Despite their eulogies to their fallen leader, members of the new government soon began to distance themselves from his ministry. Many of the changes that Perceval had opposed were gradually introduced: greater press freedom, Catholic emancipation, and parliamentary reform.

This is the same with JFK's death: all things he opposed or took time to approve were implemented fast and a few wanted to associate with his presidency.

Lord Liverpool's government did not maintain Perceval's resolution in acting against the illegal slave trade, which began to flourish as the authorities looked the other way. British historian Andro Linklater estimates that around 40,000 slaves were illegally transported from Africa to the West Indies because of lax enforcement of the law.

Soon after the United Nations declared war on the United Kingdom.

So does our first hypothesis hold water?

I think knowing that Lee Harvey Oswald had just become a father and a husband and the hard difficulties he experienced especially the deception he might have felt after realizing that the FBI pretended to give him work to fortify any prospects of compensation for his imprisonment in the US or any ill-treatment he might have suffered abroad. He might have been tempted to pull the trigger, but his grounds are weak as compared to those circumstances of the assassination of Spencer Perceval the prime minister of Britain.

His grounds are weak on their own.

This man got a wife at the time they released the movie From Russia with Love. Surely his grievances were not that pronounced. Even the visit by the FBI to see his wife wasn't aggressive enough to cause stress on his part. But the fact that he might have felt guilty for forging documents and smearing Marina when she wrote the name of Alek James Hidell on the cards for the Fair Play Cuba Committee might have made him feel guilty for putting his wife in danger of harassment by the FBI.

But you must know that Lee Harvey Oswald does not need logic to assassinate the president as much as John Bellingham did. Bellingham was a businessman; everything he did was to follow a certain pattern and logic. When accused of insanity he refuted that because what he did had logic in it.

But Oswald needed no logical grounds. He was a trained sharpshooter. Someone to just follow a command and blast whoever he was told to.

Above all the fact that he was trained to use guns might have made him quick to take action and reduce the amount of stress. It can be said that Bellingham would be expected to take action after years of trying because as a businessman there was no other option. It takes time to overcome the threshold of pain and grief to think about weapons because this is remote to him.

Oswald might have a gun at his fingertips as a way out of this trickery and deception.

So, Oswald even if he does not qualify using the above criteria might have pulled the trigger just because he can.

There are so many factors that could have made Oswald blast JFK for reasons not personal to him. He was a trained killer and needed no reason to blast JFK.

JFK's strictness and policies at the time of the heightened civil rights movements could have contributed to his death.

At the time of the shooting Oswald confessed that there were two Negros in the second level. We know that JFK delayed passing civil rights bills that could have given Oswald the guts to blast him. JFK was anti-communist that could have given Oswald fuel to blast him. There are so many reasons that Oswald could have used to justify killing him.

But we can see that so many factors are common in both killings.

1. Premeditated killings.

2. Lying in wait after establishing the presence to remove suspicion to increase the chances.

3. Warnings that are not taken seriously.

4. Purchases of two handguns.

5. Element of being abused or neglected and the need to revenge or seek redress.

6. Inability to get the redress due to further trickery worsening the situation.

7. Double blasting as an intent to kill.

8. No remote or panic after the killing with an element of gloating that I told you so now this is justice.

9. Cool and composed after the killing.

10. Denial of any hints of insanity? How can this masterpiece be

regarded as the work of a crazy man? If it was so sure the most intelligent president or prime minister could have escaped with his life. The fact that he isn't fucking breathing is an element of genius. Dame, it gives me credit. So, Bellingham thanked the judge for dismissing the insanity claim. Dame motherfuckers why take credit from me give Caesar what belongs to Caesar and give me the merits due for blasting this cruel self-centered egoistic bastard dead. But this is justice. I did humanity justice. So, walking away is the only sound judgment.

11. But above all this Beast must be the one running the show in the Oswald case. Surely, he could have not done it without it.

a] Is it fate that Ruth Paine meets Marina and takes them to Dallas Texas?

b] Is it a coincidence that the same Ruth finds a job at the Texas School Depository?

c] Is it a coincidence that the neighbor's brother Wesley Frazier works there too, the one who gave him a lift the morning of the shooting?

d] Is it a coincidence that the president was also passing through the school depository?

e] Is it a coincidence that the FBI kept interfering with his life especially after his wife gave birth to their daughter and him having no means to feed them?

f] Is it a coincidence that the Cuban embassy refused him a visa making him come back to assassinate JFK?

g] Is it a coincidence that he walks out of the Texas School Book Depository after the shooting after the cop pointed a gun at him?

h] Is it a coincidence that he ends up following John Bellingham's footsteps of blasting a prime minister or president or all this is playing according to the 1812 script?

You decide.

10

Second hypothesis.

I believe that if the Beast is behind this, then it follows too that it might have superimposed two similar cases together with one acting as a decoy or both interwoven.

The killing of JFK is also like the beheading of the King of England Charles I.

The setting.

We hypothesize that the Beast is using the same script of the execution of Charles in the screenplay of the JFK assassination.

Settings of the execution of Charles I.

1. A scaffold was erected outside the Banqueting house.

2. A block was placed so low where he would place his head that he had to prostrate as if kneeling with his head touching the ground as a way to show submission to the people by the king.

If you rotate this prostrate position of Charles I on the block 90 degrees, you have exactly the position of President JFK in the limousine and bullet trajectory pointing to the Texas School Book Depository.

3. But we know that in the assassination of JFK he was sitting in a limousine.

4. We also know that King Charles I had his head severed from the back of the head but might have impacted the ground as well as it fell after the clean cut. This will explain the jerking and movements back and to the side. This could explain why some people thought that he was shot from the front of the Grassy Knoll.

5. But we also know that the Beast will use the exact script of the execution of Charles I for the assassination of JFK.

6. So we assume the Beast might have twisted [rotated 90 degrees] the script to suit the JFK assassination but without changing any material facts.

7. We also know the route taken by the president's limousine. Can we use the angle at which the limousine motorcade turned as a guide to the position and trajectory direction of the bullets?

8. We know too that Charles I was assassinated by an axe whereas JFK was assassinated by a gun and a rifle.

This is what the beast does if you check the first weapon discovered is said to be a Mauser 7.5 rifle, but the FBI later stated that the gun was a 6.5 Italian Carcano.

9. The Zapruder film shows the president's limousine motorcade turning at an angle to the road in Dealey Plaza at an angle of 45 degrees.

10. We must superimpose the position of the execution of Charles 1 on top of the position of the assassination of JFK and rotate 45 degrees clockwise.

11. Theoretically this must match to become one position that is the same as that of JFK sitting in a limousine.

Do you know that the Dealey Plaza Grassy knoll area map is the rotation of the map in England or London? Where the Banqueting House that was part of the King's place equivalent to the place JFK was assassinated?

To make everything interesting the Texas School Book Depository corresponds to the St James Palace on the rotated map. Yes, the palace of the Queen of England at the time of the shooting.

Just on this basis, JFK was assassinated as a direct command from the queen's St James Palace.

Do you know the weeks leading to his death JFK accused Lyndon J Johnson of accusing him of treason? It started that leaflets were circulated before the assassination stating that the president had committed treason.

Wanted for Treason leaflet about JFK

This flyer, around 5,000 copies of which were distributed around Dallas in the days before President Kennedy's November 22, 1963 visit, accused Kennedy of a range of offenses, from being "lax" on Communism, to "appointing anti-Christians to Federal office," to lying to the American people about his personal life.

Wikipedia.

Treason can be committed towards a monarchy since JFK was the president, he can only be held to account on treason charges by the people of the country. But what did he do to face treason charges?

JFK was accused of putting personal goals first before people and country.

JFK is accused of embarking on wars that bring harm to the people hence his acts are contrary to the public interests as his actions were bringing harm to the people hence the treason charges.

The original leaflet reads.

This man is wanted for treasonous activities against the United States.

Betraying the constitution which he swore to uphold. He is turning the sovereignty of the US over to the communist-controlled United Nations.

He is betraying our friends Cuba, Katanga, and Portugal and befriending our enemies (Russia, Yugoslavia, Poland.)

He has been wrong on innumerable issues affecting the security of the US (United Nations -Berlin wall - missile removal - Cuba wheat deals - Tes Ban treaty, etc.)

He has been lax in enforcing communist registration laws.

He has given support and encouragement to the communist-inspired racial riots.

He has illegally invaded a sovereign state with federal troops.

He has consistently appointed anti-Christians to federal office; upholds the supreme court in its anti-Christian rulings. Aliens and now communists abound in federal office.

He has been caught in fantastic lies to the American people (including personal ones like his previous marriage and divorce.)

Wikipedia

Just like the first hypothesis for our theory to hold water the following factors must be evident in the assassination of JFK. This is because this is the working script to follow and whatever happens next is just as in the script.

The royalist losses of the English Civil War had led to Charles I's capture. Upon his trial, the High Court of Justice sentenced him to death for his tyrannical rule as King of England.

On Saturday 27 January 1649, the parliamentarian The High Court of Justice had declared Charles guilty of attempting to "uphold in himself an unlimited and tyrannical power to rule according to his will, and to overthrow the rights and liberties of the people" and he was sentenced to death by beheading. [2]

These are the same charges as those on the leaflet distributed on 21 November 1963.

On 28 January, the king was moved from the Palace of Whitehall to St James's Palace, likely to avoid the noise of the scaffold being set up outside the Banqueting House (at its rear side on the street of Whitehall). [10] Charles spent the day praying with the Bishop of London, William Juxon

Charles spent his last few days in St James's Palace, accompanied by his most loyal subjects and visited by his family. He had not seen his children for 15 months, so the parliamentarians allowed him to talk to his two youngest children, Elizabeth, and Henry, for one last time.

On 30 January, he was taken to a large black scaffold constructed in front of the Banqueting House, where he was to be executed. Charles awoke early on the day of his execution. He began dressing at 5 a.m. in fine clothes, all black, and his blue Garter sash. [18] His preparation lasted until dawn. [19] He instructed the Gentleman of the Bedchamber, Thomas Herbert, on what would be done with the few possessions he had left. [20] He requested one extra shirt from Herbert so that the crowd gathered would not see him shiver from the cold and mistake it for cowardice. At 10 a.m., Colonel Francis Hacker instructed Charles to go to Whitehall, ready for his execution. At noon, Charles drank a glass of claret wine and ate a piece of bread. The platform was draped in black and staples had been driven into the wood for ropes to be run through if Charles needed to be restrained. The execution block was so low that the king would have had to prostrate himself to place his head on the block, a submissive pose as compared to kneeling before the block.

The executioners of Charles were hidden behind face masks and wigs to prevent identification.

Just before 2 p.m., Colonel Hacker called Charles to the scaffold.

Charles came through the window of the Banqueting Hall[d] to the scaffold in what Herbert described as "the saddest sight England ever saw.

Charles saw the crowd and realized that the barrier of guards prevented the crowd from hearing any speech he would make, so he addressed his speech to Juxon and the regicide Matthew Thomlinson—the former of whom recorded the speech in shorthand.

He called himself "a martyr of the people"—claiming he would be killed for their rights.

Charles asked Juxon for his silk nightcap to put on so that the executioner would not be troubled by his hair.

The crowd could not hear the speech, owing to the many parliamentarian guards blocking the scaffold, but Charles' companion, Bishop William Juxon, recorded it in shorthand.

Charles gave Juxon his George, sash, and cloak—uttering one cryptic word: "remember".

Charles gave a few last words to Juxon, claiming his "incorruptible crown" in Heaven, and put his head on the block.

Charles laid his neck out on the block and asked the executioner to wait for his signal to behead him.

A moment passed and Charles gave the signal; the executioner beheaded him in one clean blow.

The executioner silently held up Charles' head to the spectators. He did not utter the customary cry of "Behold the head of a traitor!" either from inexperience or fear of identification.

He waited a few moments, and after giving a signal that he was ready, the anonymous executioner beheaded Charles with a single blow and held Charles' head up to the crowd silently, dropping it into the swarm of soldiers soon after.

According to the royalist Philip Henry, the crowd let out a loud groan [40]—a 17-year-old Henry writing of "such a groan [...] as I never heard before and I desire I may never hear again"

The executioner dropped the king's head into the crowd and the soldiers swarmed around it, dipping their handkerchiefs in his blood, and cutting off locks of his hair.

The body was then put in a coffin and covered with black velvet. It was temporarily placed in the king's former 'lodging chamber' within Whitehall.

Others view it as a vital step towards democracy in Britain, with the prosecutor of Charles I, John Cook, declaring that it "pronounced sentence not only against one tyrant but against tyranny itself"[6][7]

 Although he was not fundamentally anti-monarchist, he was forced to this stance when King Charles I would not recognize the legality of the court or answer the charges of tyranny against him.

The idea of trying a reigning king had no precedent; previous monarchs had been deposed but had never been brought to trial as monarchs. The High Court of Justice established by an act of the Rump Parliament consisted of 135 commissioners (all firm Parliamentarians); Cook accepted the brief to lead the prosecution.

The trial of King Charles I on charges of high treason and other high crimes began on 20 January 1649, but he refused to enter a plea, claiming that no court had jurisdiction over a monarch. [9] When Cook began to read the indictment, King Charles I twice tried to stop him by ordering him to "Hold" and twice tapping him sharply on the shoulder with his cane. Cook ignored this so King Charles then rose to speak, but Cook resumed speaking, at which point King Charles struck Cook so forcefully on the shoulder that the ornate silver tip of the cane broke off and rolled onto the floor. The King nodded to Cook to pick it up but Cook stood his ground and after a long pause, King Charles stooped to retrieve it himself. This is considered an important historical moment that was seen as symbolizing the divine monarch bowing before human law.

Thus, John Cook was tried and found guilty of high treason for his part in the trial of King Charles I. He was hanged, drawn, and quartered with the radical preacher Hugh Peters and another of the regicides on 16 October 1660. Shortly before his death, aged 52, Cook wrote to his wife Mary.

The identities of the executioner of Charles I and his assistant were never revealed to the public, with crude face masks and wigs hiding them at the execution.

They were probably only known to Oliver Cromwell and a few of his colleagues.

The clean cut on Charles' head and the fact the executioner held up Charles' head after the execution suggests the executioner was experienced in the use of an axe.

Possible executioners.

Richard Branson.

Colonel John Hewson was given the task of finding an executioner and he offered 40 soldiers the position of executioner or assistant in exchange for £100 and quick promotion, though none came forward immediately. [52] It has been suggested that one of these soldiers later accepted the job, the most probable candidate among the men being Hulet. Shortly after the execution, Hulet received a prominent and swift promotion and he was not seen to be present on the day of Charles' execution.

His alibi consisted of the claim he was imprisoned on the day for refusing the position, though this seems to conflict with his promotion soon after. [53] William Hulet was tried as the executioner in October 1660, upon the Restoration, and he was sentenced to death for his supposed part in the execution. This sentence was soon overturned and Hulet was pardoned after some exculpatory evidence was presented to the judge. [54]

Wikipedia

The most likely candidate for the executioner was Richard Brandon, the common hangman at the time of Charles' execution

John Cook or Cooke (baptized 18 September 1608[1] – 16 October 1660) [2][3] was the first Solicitor General of the English Commonwealth and led the prosecution of Charles I. Following the Restoration, Cook was convicted of regicide and hanged, drawn, and quartered on 16 October 1660. He is considered an international legal icon and progenitor of international criminal law for being the first lawyer to prosecute a head of state for crimes against his people.

Before he was appointed prosecutor, he had established a reputation as a radical lawyer and an Independent.

Incorruptible Crown[edit]

The Incorruptible Crown is also known as the Imperishable Crown, and is referenced in 1 Corinthians 9:25.[2] This epistle, written by Paul of Tarsus, deems this crown "imperishable" in order "to contrast it with the temporal awards Paul's contemporaries pursued".[8] It is therefore given to those

individuals who demonstrate "self-denial and perseverance".

Wikipedia.

The Assassination of JFK using the Execution Script of King Charles I of England 30 January 1649

Setting Grassy Knoll / Dealey Plaza representing The Banqueting House. [see maps enclosed]

Where the School Book Depository represents St James Palace

The Cast Jack Frederick Kennedy as King Charles I of England.

Lyndon Baines Johnson playing Oliver Cromwell.

A 2003 Gallup poll indicated that nearly 20% of Americans suspected Lyndon B. Johnson of being involved in the assassination of Kennedy. [425] Critics of the Warren Commission have accused Johnson of plotting the assassination because he "disliked" the Kennedys and feared that he would be dropped from the Democratic ticket for the 1964 election

Johnson perpetrated the assassination of Kennedy

John Connally playing John Bradshaw.

Jacqueline Kennedy Onassis playing Henrietta Maria.

Lee Harvey Oswald playing Richard Brandon.

Richard Brandon died 20 June 1649) [a] was the common executioner of London from 1639 to 1649, who inherited his role from his father Gregory Brandon and was sometimes known as Young Gregory. [2] Richard Brandon is often named as the executioner of Charles I, though the executioner's identity is not known. [3

The executioner and his assistant were hidden behind false wigs and beards, with crude masks covering their faces.

Wikipedia.

Oswald could be the assassin as he had two Selective service system cards with the same face but two different names: Lee Harvey Oswald and Alek James Hidell. This could be what this refers to.

Here the script has been matched.

Eventually, a man and his assistant agreed to carry out the task - but on the condition that they could wear masks to protect their identity.

In 1660, a man called William Hulet was put on trial for carrying out the deed. One witness, Richard Gittens, claimed that he had recognized Hulet's voice at the execution when the executioner had asked Charles to forgive him. However, several witnesses for the defense claimed that Richard Brandon had privately admitted on several occasions to beheading Charles. William Cox, for example, claimed that he had heard Brandon admit to Lord Capel – who was about to be executed – that he had carried out the deed. According to Cox, Brandon admitted that he was paid a considerable sum of money (£30) for executing the king. Hulet was found not guilty at his trial and released.

Wikipedia

The executioner's assistant is also unknown. One opinion is that he was a Parliamentarian named George Joyce. Joyce made his name by seizing Charles at Holdenby House and bringing him to Newmarket, probably with Oliver Cromwell's support and knowledge. The principal evidence against Joyce came from an astrologer called William Lilly. Lilly described a dinner he attended with a Parliamentary Committee. At the same dinner was Robert Spavin, Cromwell's secretary. Lilly claimed that the sole discussion at the dinner was the execution of Charles, which had only recently taken place. One person at the dinner claimed that the executioner was "the Common Hangman" (a reference to Richard Brandon's official title). However, Spavin claimed that the executioner's assistant was Lieutenant Colonel Joyce and that only Cromwell, Ireton and he knew this.

Some suggest Thomas Fairfax and Oliver Cromwell had personally executed Charles and the precise identity of the executioner remains unknown. The execution of Charles I was done expertly, with a single clean cut to Charles' neck, possibly suggesting that the executioner was experienced, and pointing towards someone like Brandon who had much pride in his use of an axe. [14][15] He is also reported to have received £30 around the time of the execution. [16] He had also executed other royalists before Charles and after, including Thomas Wentworth, William Laud, and Lord Capel, indicating few moral qualms over executing political criminals. [17] Despite this, a contemporary letter reports that he refused £200 to kill the king,[18] and he continually denied having committed the act, even until his death in June 1649.

This tract claimed that Brandon had been paid £30 for his actions and returned home from the execution under cover of night, at 6 o'clock. [23]

Wikipedia.

JD Tippit the policemen

Parkland Hospital is where five people associated with JFK were pronounced dead.

John F Kennedy himself

Lee Harvey Oswald

Jack Ruby who later killed Oswald

Abraham Zapruder the man who filmed the assassination

Jean Hill eyewitness as the woman in red.

First English civil war [Civil rights Movement of the 1960s]

JFK Assassination and link to Charles I's treason and hanging.

First, we look at the similarities between methods and acts.

i] Horse-drawn carts to transport prisoners to places of execution. Exactly like a modern-day open limousine.

ii] Public and open with people given vacations to watch.

iii] The victims knew they were going to die and were unable to do anything about it, instead encouraged to die like a man.

iv] A clean shot to sever the head as an execution method.

vii] Real executioner disguised forever to protect his identity. Killing the king or President is a treason charge too.

The Vice President the Electronic Transfer.

viii]Often paraded in public as a way of raising money by the local councils.

ix] The second beast is the stagecoach of such an event with the victim the king or president previously hacked illegally by doctors or hospitals with ambulances running around making horns (sirens) frightening him and threatening his family.

X] VIP seats accumulate great prices.

Xi] Surgeons and hospital staff wait for the corpse to do an experiment and research.

xii] The victim was not even given a chance to talk to watch the first bullet severing JFK's vocal codes. Charles I, have not been given a chance to talk.

xiii] The trial setting resembled an open limousine with two judges in front-facing Charles I John Bradshaw and Thomas Grey.

xiv] We know the judges wore a helmet in case of assassination attempts. We also have the police and armed forces given orders to stand down by the court in Charles's case and here to do nothing but watch. The question on your mind right now is why JFK and how does he compare to an English king?

The US and the British both practice common law where the idea I discussed above legal precedence stems from. Bear in mind what I said about legal precedence. If President Y steps in the shoes of President X and carries out the same acts as President X and because the two cases are directly in point one can go back to this precedent case and deduce that President Y simply is doing the same as President X, he might suffer the same consequences as President X. If Charles I, a king, very feared during those days could easily be killed by poor common people, people with no land or riches just because he committed high treason, what more on behalf of a President who is regarded as crooked? I think the reader to see the implication of the English law to modern-day events must establish the direct in-point hypothesis between Charles I and JFK.

"Direct in Point" Charles I versus JFK case.

It is a fact that the Warren Commission found out that a flier was distributed days before JFK's visit accusing him of treason and stating that he was wanted.

The Warren Commission reported that 5 000 fliers stating that JFK was wanted for treason were distributed days before his visit and these leaflets were left on windscreens and in shops. The flier had seven grounds namely: The flier is written: This man is wanted for treasonous activities against the United States:

Betraying the Constitution (which he swore to uphold): He is turning the sovereignty of the U.S. Over to the communist-controlled United Nations. He is betraying our friends (Cuba, Katanga, Portugal) and befriending our enemies (Russia, Yugoslavia, Poland).

He has been WRONG on innumerable issues affecting the security of the US. (United Nations Berlin Wall-Missile removal- Cuba-Wheat Deals-Test ban Treaty etc.)

He has been lax in enforcing Communist Registration laws.

He has given support and encouragement to the Communist-inspired racial riots.

He has illegally invaded a sovereign State with federal troops. 6] He has consistently appointed Anti-Christians to Federal office. Upholds the Supreme Court in Anti-Christian rulings. Aliens and known Communists abounded in Federal Offices/

7] He has been caught in fantastic lies to the American people, including personal ones like his previous marriage and divorce.

The Warren Commission acknowledges that JFK was aware of the treason leaflets that had appeared in the Dallas newspaper a day before he visited Dallas. He displayed dismay at being portrayed as such as in the old-style western movies where a poster is distributed with the Wanted Dead or Alive for criminals. JFK himself in his diary wrote that Lyndon Johnson was accusing him of treason and being stupid just a few days before he was.

Assassinated. Just like Charles I, was seen advancing personal agendas and taking the country into a dangerous road putting lives at risk and engaging in wars that were not of national interest. Just like Charles I, his personal life is brought into question regarding his marriage and dealings with Marilyn Monroe. He is accused of siding with non-Christians. Charles was accused of marrying a catholic and forcing a catholic prayer book on the Scots. JFK was accused of allowing non-Christians in the federal system. His acts regarding Cuba are seen as acts violating the constitution something, he swore to protect, and as such guilty as charged. Here is that idea again of precedence? We see him accused of treason by Johnson. This should be viewed in the context that Lyndon Johnson was ridiculed by JFK and his brother as the man to succeed him in office. This might have been an act of revenge on personal grounds rather than real charges of treason but that won't change the fact that just because of this and the fact that legal precedence existed, and the cases seemed to be direct in point one could have said that JFK could suffer the same fate as Charles I of England? We know the US and the British share common law, customary, and ancestors. Look at the hangings at Tyburn as discussed above. That can also explain the fliers of treason distributed days before his assassination. He might have been cornered and blackmailed by the second beast, the ambulance, doctors, and hospital who might have illegally hacked him during an operation to check his eyes and the problems he experienced during his political career. The second beast used him for personal agendas. We know that he was against the enemy within. Could he have been talking about the second beast, hacking him and remotely tampering with his system controlling him, and threatening his family? A system is common with kings and monarchies. We have proof that he lived in Britain when his father was an ambassador to the UK. Somehow, he might have been in the presence of the second beast. A very common practice in England or Poland where everyone is hacked and assigned a serial number. Don't forget that the British "liberated the Poles" might have adopted the system from Hitler but still practiced the same although underground. Just an assumption I leave the reader.

Extracts from the Vice President. The Electronic Transfer by Carolinadeivid [My other penname]

During the trial Charles, I argued that the parliament was a threat to the freedoms and liberties of the people rather than him. On January 24, 1649 thirty-three witnesses gave accounts of the charges of high treason and his involvement. They gave accounts of his involvement in wars, his ordering of the continued wars, and his killings of the people. On 26 January the commissioner declared Charles I as guilty. They noted that he had become an enemy of the people and such a cruel and oppressive ruler. Therefore, the charges brought against him were fitting too. On 27 January Bradshaw gave a chilling 40 minutes account of how Charles I had broken all laws putting the country and his people in danger by embarking on stupid and dangerous wars, getting people killed needlessly, and as such guilty of betraying the people he is supposed to protect. (reminiscent of JFK when accused by Lyndon, remember the art of prediction and precedent discussed above?).

Bradshaw rejected the king's assertion that a king is a divine entity appointed by God and as such is not answerable to man. He was appointed by God all his acts were acts on behalf of God and no man can be expected to question God's decisions. Bradshaw, therefore, had no authority to pass judgment on him. Bradshaw contended that even the king was under the law and that parliament was the one who passed the laws and the judgment and as such he can be tried using the law and judgment passed accordingly. He went on to declare Charles I guilty as charged and sentenced him to death by hanging. Bradshaw had argued in detail that it was true the people owed allegiance to the king, but he also emphasized that the King had broken that agreement, that the bond between king and subject was broken as he had waged war on his people. This meant that the sacred bond was broken as he had lost the privilege of their right to allegiance. Charles, I was not allowed to speak but was led away straight away without the chance to present his case, something he didn't expect. Bear this in mind as this will explain the shooting of JFK first in the throats we go into more detail. It is also noteworthy to quickly look at the Rump parliament and how it orchestrated the hanging of Charles I's supporters.

The Death Warrant of Charles I

At the High Court of Justice for the trying and judging of Charles Stuart, King of England, Jan. 29, Anno Domini 1648.

Whereas Charles Stuart, King of England, is, and standeth convicted, attainted, and condemned of high treason, and other high crimes; and sentence upon Saturday last was pronounced against him by this Court, to be put to death by the severing of his head from his body; of which sentence, execution vet remaineth to be done: these are therefore to will and require you to see the said sentence executed in the open street before Whitehall, upon the morrow, being the thirtieth day of this instant month of January, between the hours of ten in the morning and five in the afternoon of the same day, with full effect. And for so doing this shall be your sufficient warrant. And these are to require all officers, soldiers, and others, the good people of this nation of England, to be assisting unto you in this service. [emphasis added]

The trial of Charles I was a public open affair. This was a common English practice in high treason cases.

Crimes of King Charles 1 of England.

I need to address the main reasons why Charles I was accused of high treason before looking at capital punishment.

His beliefs in the Divine Rights of Kings are a topic I have already covered above. Charles, I came into conflict with parliament as they tried but in vain to quash his royal prerogative. He believed kings were above all earthly judges and considered himself able to rule using his conscience. He levied taxes without the consent of parliament which he saw fitting as the sovereign entity it was not required of him to seek approval from Parliament. In 1642 Charles was suspected of the presence of enemies within (reminiscent of JFK's enemies within speech) close English members of parliament who had colluded with the Scots to overthrow him and regarded these as enemies of the monarchy and charged them with high treason issuing arrest warrants. Parliament refused to cooperate with him and protected its members as the message leaked and they escaped. Charles I's actions to enter the House of Commons breaking established privileges and rules that no king was to enter the House of Commons caused a rift between parliament and the king, especially the fact that he had arrest warrants for five members of parliament. (striking similarities to what JFK did appointing his brother as the Attorney General was such an act similar to what king Charles I did) This challenge meant mistrust and set the chain of events leading to his downfall. Parliament went on to accuse Charles I of using the monarchy's privileges for his agendas instead of for the good of the public. Charles, I had failed under parliamentary laws and was perceived to have abused and failed to carry out his command responsibilities to safeguard the interest of the people he was supposed to protect.

Extracts from The Vice President the Electronic Transfer

Command responsibility.

Any superior in a position of trust must act, a duty to do

something within a reasonable time frame to safeguard the interest of those who are under him. His sole aim should be to safeguard the interest of the people he is supposed to protect and not to consider his agendas first at the expense of the people he is supposed to protect. The superior acquires liability by default or omission. The superior cannot claim ignorance because he is aware of the situation and as such is liable as he is expected to act to avoid such crimes of torture, for example, to have happened. The superior can prevent such criminal conduct but fails to do so or takes a long time to act. The superior failed to take any corrective action and to punish those involved. Back to Charles I, was accused of failing to act during the wars that saw murders, damages, and desolation as 300 000 of the population perished during the wars. Deaths that were viewed as unnecessary and deaths that could have been prevented had Charles, I carried out command responsibility as required by the law. To Charles I the illegality of the trials was unquestionable. The people trying him had used force to bring him there and as such had no proper authority to try him especially since he was not answerable to any man but to God himself. The courts refused to subscribe to the doctrine of sovereign immunity stating that such a privilege was not to be abused and in case that occurred parliament had powers to bring the king to justice.

Execution of Charles I outside Banqueting House. 30 January 1649.

He left the king's Palace St James and headed to Whitehall where a platform was erected in front of the Banqueting House to execute him. Ranks of soldiers surrounded him and separated him from the public. Charles, I acknowledged his failings to support and save Thomas Wentworth 1st Earl of Stafford who had previously supported him and who advocated for him in the strengthening the king's bargaining position against parliament a crime that saw his death. Parliament accused him of treason and king Charles I even signed his death warrant. After delivering his speech two hours afternoon he stretched out his hands to signal that he was ready the executioner went on to behead him severing his head with a clean strike which was later confirmed by the examiners and surgeons after that it was the strike of an experienced executioner. The executioner for fear of appraisals was disguised covering his face and did not even speak in case someone identifies him. The idea was that killing a king was treason and some would take revenge, or they would find it fitting to revenge whether he was a bad person or not. One Richard Brandon who was the executioner at the time was approached and asked if he was the king's executioner, but he denied any involvement despite a $200 bribe. Others have been associated with the King's execution, but no one came forward to accept responsibility. Public executions of treason traitors meant the displaying of their heads and Charles I was no different as his head was displayed. After the execution, the head was attached back to the body and his body was preserved.

To Col. Francis Hacker, Col. Huncks, and Lieut-Col. Phayre, and to every one of them. Given under our hands and seals.

JOHN BRADSHAW. THOMAS GREY. OLIVER CROMWELL.

[* * * 59 names in all.]

[http://law2.umkc.edu/faculty/projects/ftrials/charlesIlinks.html]

An open oxcart was used to transport the prisoners from Newgate to Tyburn for hanging. The authorities encouraged those to be executed to 'die in style' to dress their best and show no fear at all. They were encouraged to act like it was another day to give the audience a great show. The people were known to applaud a fearless death and jeer any fear-torn prisoners. In short, prisoners were transported to Tyburn in the 1600s to the 1800s in an open horse-drawn cart (what comes to your mind? Modern-day open limousines? Picture JFK being paraded and being poked by the doctors and nurses and the ambulances sounding their sirens threatening his wife and kids and pressuring him to put on a show and die in style. We know he might have been hacked during the operation without consent remember the second beast in Revelations 13?) Newgate to Tyburn was approximately 3 miles (4,8km). Streets were often lined up with onlookers making such a journey last more than 3 hours in an open horse-drawn cart. The only allowed stop for the prisoners to drink strong alcohol was at a place called the Bowl in St Giles.

The hanging square was often crowded with people shouting and applauding others jeering. The rich would pay for the best seats to witness the execution. Tyburn was more than a place to carry out capital punishment. It was a place for social gathering as well, just like the Roman Colosseum was for entertainment and funds collection, as was Tyburn. Tyburn was a source of corpses for the hungry surgeons and doctors who operated on the corpse as soon as they were executed. This is true in JFK's assassination when the doctors fought to be the ones carrying out the autopsy. The removal of parts from the corpse for study and research can also explain why JFK's brain went missing after. Coincidence or precedence? You decide at the end of the report.

Characteristics of public executions at Tyburn that are of interest to the report.

Executions attracted a lot of people and this was in the open and generally regarded as entertainment for the spectators. This is synonymous with the executions of Christians during the Roman empire with the rich paying large sums to reserve special VIP seats. It was also a way of collecting and raising money for the local councils while at the same time providing unequaled entertainment. There was a fee to be paid to secure the elevated stands to have the best view at Tyburn. People were given public vacations to attend and see the executions.

The idea throughout this book is that a foreign nation in the form of the Beast II forced protection in that it created a situation that exposed the weakness of a country and then provided solutions to the problem created. It then goes on to put demands in return for its protection. So, it's like blackmail. It created the problem itself and then prescribed a solution. But is this real protection or what has been referred to as grooming? More precisely, it's like being on death row. Being groomed to be killed. Given a false sense of security then killed when you least expected. Look at the JFK case. He spoke about enemies within. Even on the day he died, he talked about the threat of being shot. He knew someone had pretended to give him protection. Then exploited him. Parading him all over before executing him when he least suspected. This is a very common tactic that goes back to the Tyburn era in England. Those about to be hanged were asked to wear their best before being paraded. They were asked to put on a show and not to show fear but to die in-style one might say. Just like in the Rome era with the execution of Christians. They were paraded and a lot of people would attend and those with money paid for VIP seats. In England, in Tyburn, this was a way for the councils to raise funds. This is true even years after as in 1629. When King Charles I had been tried for treason and found guilty, he was told that he would be executed. The day before the execution he asked for two shirts and the reason being that he did not want people to see him shivering because of the cold in case the people mistaken it for fear. I explained throughout volumes I & II that the Beast II is working very hard marking people with marks and digital serial numbers and advanced tools as revealed in Revelations. We know animals like dogs and cats are now given tags for identification and electric collars for controlling them and guiding them as a form of

119

protection. They give people a false sense of security.

Extracts from: The Vice President the Electronic Transfer. II The Death Trap.

It is because it's not protection, it's grooming as someone on death row and in the end just surprising you. The Beast II's job with the help of the dragon who causes fire everywhere is to kill as many people as he can. Human rights and the years of enlightenment have hindered Beast II's progress in imitating God.

The Warren Commission concluded that Oswald, an employee at the depository, shot and mortally wounded President Kennedy from a sixth-floor window on the building's south-eastern corner; Kennedy died at Parkland Memorial Hospital.

Lee Harvey Oswald, after the assassination of John F. Kennedy, denied he was responsible for the murder, and stated: "No, they are taking me in because I lived in the Soviet Union. I'm just a patsy.

patsy (n.)

"fall guy, the victim of a deception,"

https://www.etymonline.com/word/patsy

Jack Leon Ruby (born Jacob Leon Rubenstein; April 25, 1911 – January 3, 1967) was an American nightclub owner and alleged associate of the Chicago Outfit who murdered Lee Harvey Oswald on November 24, 1963, two days after Oswald was accused of the assassination of President John F. Kennedy. A Dallas jury found Ruby guilty of murdering Oswald and sentenced him to death. Ruby's conviction was later repealed, and he was to be granted a new trial; however, he became ill in prison and died of a pulmonary embolism from lung cancer on January 3, 1967.

Background factual material part of the Warren Commission notes

… …..

To be continued in Volume II when I concluded all the facts and give you exactly what we think happened.

I hope we have shown you a more satisfactory alternative to the story of the authorities oh what happened on 22 November 1963.

At least this is the only explanation that answers and debunks all conspiracy theories.

This is because this is a three-crimes-in-one. That unless if you combine all the crimes as one you will never find out what really happened on that afternoon in Dealey Plaza, Texas.

But we decoded the myths and I think you agree that so far this is the best explanation.

The Beast is the one acting like a film director, controlling the lives of people. Putting people through tough times so that they do what it wants.

If a hostage; someone being forced to do what he is doing forcefully or unfairly goes on to kill. Can the blame be apportioned to the hostage taker, the Beast?

I think our task is to prove that all these people are doing what they are due to the hacking or commands by the Beast.

But who is the Beast?

GET VOLUME II STRAIGHT AWAY.

ABOUT DAVID GOMADZA

The First Global President of The World.

www.twofuture.world

info@twofuture.world

Evolution of Democracy. The Assassination of President JFK SOLVED.